revision guides

PracticePapers
KS3 Maths

S.10

Attainment Targets

School subjects are divided into separate sections of work known as attainment targets. Details of the Mathematics attainment targets are given below.

In each attainment target, or section of study, students may be working at different levels, according to their abilities. The levels each have a reference number. For example, a child may achieve level 4 in English at the end of primary schooling (the end of KS2). By the end of the key stage tests in Year 9, this child may have progressed to level 5, 6 or 7 within the same area of study. Most school subjects are divided into several attainment targets (ATs). For example:

Subject	number of ATs (= sections)
English	3
Mathematics	4
Science	4
History	1

The overall subject level achieved by a student will be calculated from the separate levels for each of the attainment targets. For example, in English, a child achieving levels 4, 5 and 6 in the three attainment targets, will be awarded the average, level 5. In Mathematics the situation is more complicated since the attainment targets do not carry equal weighting; some are regarded as more important. In the case of Mathematics, the overall subject level is not a simple average score.

Mathematics National Tests at KS3 (the Year 9 SATs)

The National Curriculum in Mathematics is divided into four sections or four attainment targets:

* Ma1 Using and applying Mathematics
This covers using mathematics in practical situations.
For example, students might study the number of concrete slabs needed to pave a patio. They might investigate which shape of slab is most economic for the task.

* Ma2 Number and algebra
Students continue their studies on using numbers, e.g. fractions, decimals, percentages, ratios, etc. They also learn to solve problems using algebra.

* Ma3 Shape, space and measures
Students study 2-D and 3-D shapes. They estimate and measure distances and angles accurately. They study simple trigonometry and use this and Pythagoras' theorem to solve problems.

* Ma4 Handling data
Students learn to collect data and record it. They then learn how to represent data in frequency diagrams, pie charts and line graphs. They learn to interpret graphs. They also study probability.

More details of the programme of study can be found on the National Curriculum website www.nc.uk.net.

Each of the four attainment targets in Mathematics (Ma1 to Ma4) is given equal importance.

This is how they are assessed.

Attainment target	Assessment method
Ma1	Teacher assessment and in the National Test in Year 9. Questions on Ma1 are usually set within the context of one of the other attainment targets.
Ma2	National Test in Year 9.
Ma3	National Test in Year 9.
Ma4	National Test in Year 9.

The Year 9 Mathematics tests are available in three different ranges of levels, known as tiers. The least demanding papers are Tier 3–5 covering levels 3 to 5 of the National Curriculum. The most demanding papers are Tier 5–7 covering levels 5 to 7 of the National Curriculum. The Tier 4–6 papers consist of the most difficult questions on the Tiers 3–5 papers and the least difficult questions from the Tiers 5–7 papers.

In each tier one paper (Paper 1) is a non-calculator paper and one paper (Paper 2) allows you to use a calculator. For the calculator paper make sure your calculator is working and you know how to use it. You need only a simple calculator and not a scientific calculator.

In addition you should have:

- a pen, pencil and rubber
- a ruler (30 cm)
- an angle measurer
- a pair of compasses
- tracing paper
- a mirror (for symmetry questions).

In addition to the written papers you need to do a Mental Mathematics test. There are two in this book – Test 1 is for use with the Tier 3–5 papers and Test 2 with the Tier 5–7 papers. Those taking the Tier 4–6 papers could try either of the tests. You will need the help of a parent, brother or sister or friend to help you do this. They will need a watch or clock which shows seconds. They will read out each question in turn and you will have a short period of time either 5 seconds, 10 seconds or 15 seconds to write down your answer on the Answer Sheet.

Students are entered by their school for the tier that matches their recent performance in Mathematics. Each paper contains questions from all of the Mathematics attainment targets. Students have to take both Paper 1 and Paper 2 of the same tier, say Tier 3–5.

How can I prepare for the National Tests?

This book has been designed to give you the best possible chance of success in the Year 9 National Tests. The way to find out if you really understand a topic is simple – try to answer questions on that topic.

This book has been written in order to:

- cover all of the main topics you are likely to meet in the examination
- give you questions that are very similar in style to the Year 9 tests
- give you detailed answers and advice about how to achieve top marks
- give you a choice of levels to try, just like the real examinations:
  Paper 1 levels 3–5 or levels 4–6 or levels 5–7
  Paper 2 levels 3–5 or levels 4–6 or levels 5–7
- give you practice taking a Mental Mathematics test
- encourage you to improve your performance by trying the test papers more than once.

How should I use this book?

The way to get the most from this book is very simple. Follow these steps:

- *Step 1* Choose a topic, for example angles or simple equations.

- *Step 2* Spend 15 minutes revising the topic first.
  Revision could use
  – your class notes
  – your textbook
  – the web.
  You might check the examples you have done in class.

- *Step 3* Scan through the questions in this book until you find one on the same topic.

- *Step 4* Try the question.

- *Step 5* Look at the mark scheme for the question. Were there any problems? Read the answers and the advice given. Next time you will be able to gain full marks on a question like this.

Revision is very, very boring. The trick is to use your time effectively so that it does not take up all your free time.

   Successful revision = a little and often

Concentrate your efforts on the topics you find difficult.

Taking the full test and finding your national level

When the real Year 9 National Test is getting near, try a complete Paper 1 and Paper 2. Choose more than one level if you like. Perhaps start with the Tier 4–6 papers. If you do well on these then try the Tier 5–7 papers. If you were disappointed with your results on the Tier 4–6 papers, try the Tier 3–5 papers.

- Write your answers.
- Use the mark scheme to find your total score.
- Add your scores for Papers 1, 2 and a Mental Maths test.
- Check the mark scheme table on page 96 to see the level you have achieved.

Remember the results you get are only a guide. On the day you can do better or worse. However, if you have the confidence of having completed the questions and scored well this will help you.

Good luck

Tier 3-5

Paper 1: Calculator **not** allowed
Paper 2: Calculator allowed

Remember

- Each test is 1 hour long.

- You **must not** use a calculator for any question in Paper 1.

- You may use a calculator for any question in Paper 2.

- You will need: pen, pencil, rubber, ruler, protractor, a pair of compasses, tracing paper and mirror (optional).

- Each test starts with easier questions.

- Try to answer all the questions.

- Write your answers and working on the test paper – do not use any rough paper. Marks may be awarded for working.

- Check your work carefully.

- Ask your teacher if you are not sure what to do.

1. (a) Tom asked 30 pupils what they eat at dinnertime.

15 pupils have school dinners.
10 pupils bring sandwiches.
5 pupils have no dinner at all.

He draws a table of results using the symbol (●) to represent 5 pupils.

Complete the pictogram to show the results.

School dinners	○ ○ ○ ○ ○ ○ ○ ○ ○ ○ ○ ○ ○ ○ ○
Sandwiches	○ ○ ○ ○ ○ ○ ○ ○ ○ ○
No dinner	○ ○ ○ ○ ○

2 marks

(b) Amy asked some pupils how much homework they received in one night.
She drew a bar chart to show the results.

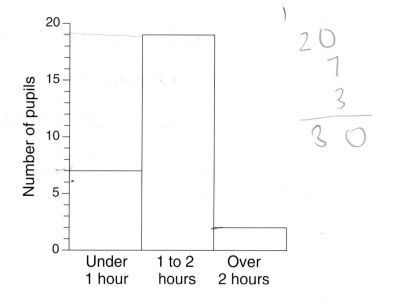

How many pupils did Amy ask?

_____ 30 _____ pupils   *1 mark*

Total Score

maximum 3 marks

2. Three thermometers A, B and C are shown below.

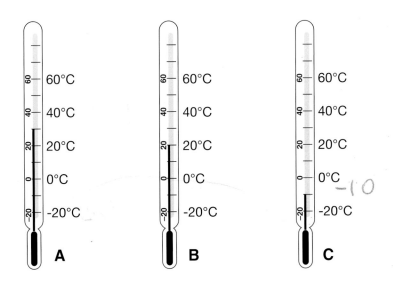

(a) What temperature is thermometer A showing?

_____30_____ °C   *2 marks*

(b) What is the difference in temperature shown by thermometers A and C?

_____40_____ °C   *2 marks*

(c) Gemma is in a very hot room. Which thermometer is she using?

_____A_____   *2 marks*

3. Here are some number cards:

Fill in the boxes using the number cards.

(a) $\boxed{9} \times \boxed{4} = 36$ *2 marks*

(b) $\boxed{10} \div \boxed{2} = \boxed{5}$ *3 marks*

(c) $(\boxed{4} + \boxed{5}) \times \boxed{9} = 81$ *3 marks*

Total Score ☐

4. The quadrilateral ABCD is shown below on a centimetre square grid.

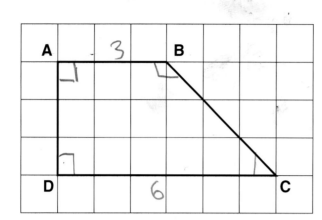

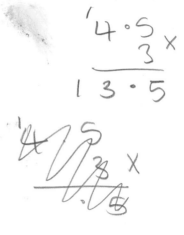

(a) Without measuring the angles, complete the table below.

Angle	Size
A	90°
B	135°
C	45°
D	90°

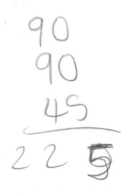

3 marks

(b) What is the area of shape ABCD?

_____13.5 cm2_____   *2 marks*

5. A mirror is placed on the following letters as shown by the dotted line on the letter A.

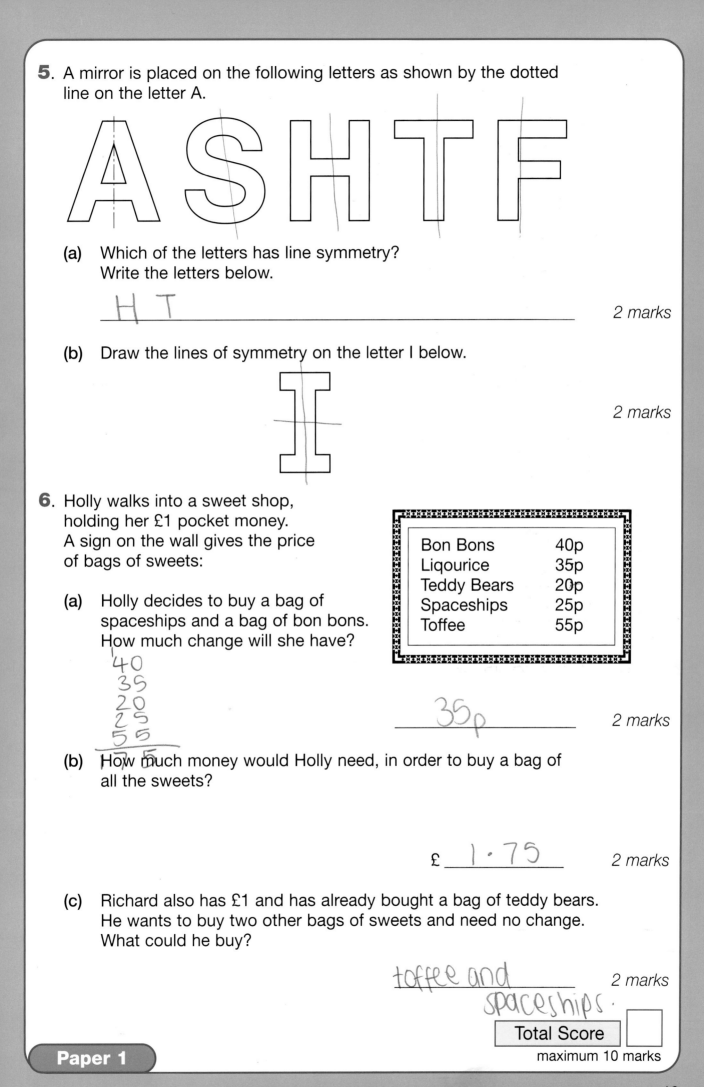

    (a)   Which of the letters has line symmetry?
          Write the letters below.

         H T   *2 marks*

    (b)   Draw the lines of symmetry on the letter I below.

                                                                 2 marks

6. Holly walks into a sweet shop, holding her £1 pocket money. A sign on the wall gives the price of bags of sweets:

Bon Bons	40p
Liqourice	35p
Teddy Bears	20p
Spaceships	25p
Toffee	55p

    (a)   Holly decides to buy a bag of spaceships and a bag of bon bons. How much change will she have?

        40
        35
        20
        25
        55
        75   35p   *2 marks*

    (b)   How much money would Holly need, in order to buy a bag of all the sweets?

                            £ 1·75   *2 marks*

    (c)   Richard also has £1 and has already bought a bag of teddy bears. He wants to buy two other bags of sweets and need no change. What could he buy?

                 toffee and spaceships.   *2 marks*

Total Score

7. Fill in the missing numbers in the patterns:

(a) 20 , 40, 60, 80 , 100   *2 marks*

(b) 1, 1, 2, 3, 5, 7 , 9   *2 marks*

(c) 1, 2, 4, 8, 12 , 16   *2 marks*

(d) 80, 40, 20, 10 , -10 , -20   *3 marks*

8. Here are 5 numbers:

0.47   0.047   47   477.0   0.4070

(a) Which number is the same as 47 ÷ 1000?

_____   *1 mark*

(b) Arrange the numbers in order from smallest to largest.

0·047, 0·4070, _____   *2 marks*

0 . 4 7 0 . 0
0 . 0 4 7 0
. 4 7 0 0
4 4 7 . 0 0 0 0
0 . 4 0 7 0

Total Score

maximum 12 marks

9. Kieran thinks of numbers between 1 and 20.

Which number is Kieran thinking of in each of the following?

(a) An even, prime number. _____ *1 mark*

(b) A multiple of 6 and greater than 13. _____ *1 mark*

(c) A square number which is a multiple of 3. _____ *1 mark*

(d) An odd factor of 26 other then 1. _____ *1 mark*

10. Below is the grid of a map:

It can be split into 3 areas that make up a town on the map.

    A   **B**   **C**

(a) Which area is $\frac{1}{8}$ of the grid? _____ *1 mark*

(b) What fraction of the grid do areas
B and C make up when
put together? _____ *2 marks*

Total Score ☐

Paper 1   maximum 7 marks

15

11. Jasmine and Kumar each hold a die.

(a) Jasmine throws the die. What is the probability that the die lands on an even number?

_____ *1 mark*

(b) They decide to add the scores on the dice.

How many ways can they make a total score of 7?
Show your working out by giving the different ways.

_____ *2 marks*

Which total scores have the lowest chance of being thrown?

_____ *2 marks*

12. 5 people queue for a roller coaster ride.
Their ages are shown below:

18 years   12 years   26 years   10 years   34 years

(a) What is the age range of the 5 people?

_____ years   *1 mark*

(b) What is the mean age? Show your working out.

_____ years   *2 marks*

(c) A sixth person joins the queue and the mean age rises to 22 years.
How old is the sixth person? Show your working out.

_____ years   *2 marks*

13. Each square is 1 cm².

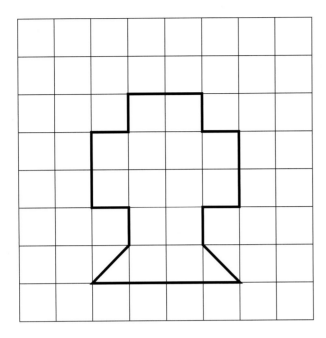

(a) What is the area of this shape?

_____ cm²   *1 mark*

(b) Draw its line of symmetry.   *1 mark*

(c) Draw a rectangle around it with a perimeter of 26 cm.   *2 marks*

Total Score

maximum 4 marks

14. Adam's father is 48 years old and his brother Graham is half his father's age.
How old will Graham be when Adam's father is 60?
Show your working out.

_____   *3 marks*

15. Show your working out when solving the following.
Find the value of:

(a) B, when $N = 40$ and $G = 25$
$N = G + B$

$B =$ _____   *2 marks*

(b) T when $R = 10$ and $C = 20$
$R = T \div C$

$T =$ _____   *2 marks*

(c) A when $T = 3$ and $R = 5$
$2(T + R)^2 = A$

$A =$ _____   *2 marks*

Total Score ☐

16. (a) What is the volume of the cuboid shown below?
Show your working out.

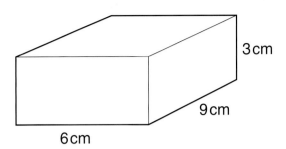

3 cm

9 cm

6 cm

_____ cm³   *2 marks*

(b) What is the surface area of the cuboid?
Show your working out.

_____ cm²   *2 marks*

(c) If the cuboid is a container, how many 3 cm cubes would fit inside it?
Show your working out.

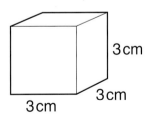

3 cm

3 cm

3 cm

_____   *1 mark*

Total Score [ ]

maximum 5 marks

17. **(a)** Give the value of these squares:

$3^2 =$ _____ $6^2 =$ _____ $13^2 =$ _____ *3 marks*

(b) Give the value of these square roots:

$\sqrt{49} =$ _____ $\sqrt{64} =$ _____ $\sqrt{225} =$ _____ *3 marks*

18. **(a)** Use compasses to construct a triangle with sides 7 cm, 6 cm and 5 cm. One side has been drawn for you.

_____
7 cm

2 marks

(b) Measure each angle of the triangle and label them in your drawing. *3 marks*

Total Score

1. (a) Name the shape on the grid shown below.

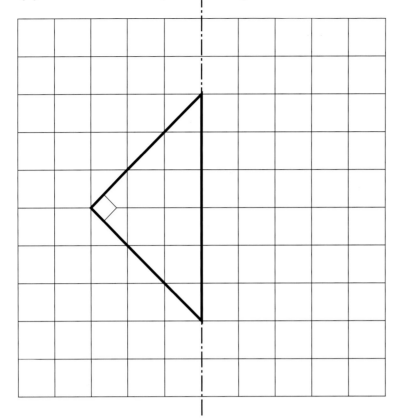

_____ *1 mark*

(b) Using the dotted line as a line of symmetry, reflect the shape and draw the reflection. *1 mark*

(c) Name the completed shape.   _____ *1 mark*

2. Below are four number cards:

(a) Which two cards will make the following true?

☐ + ☐ = 6   *2 marks*

(b) Place the cards in order, smallest to largest.

_____ *2 marks*

(c) Which three cards will make the following true?

☐ + ☐ + ☐ = –1   *3 marks*

Total Score ☐

3. Amina's class counted traffic passing the school for one hour at two different times on the same day. The results are shown here:

	Time A	Time B
Cars	22	35
Lorries	8	12
Vans	12	16
Motorbikes	5	15
Other	7	5

(a) Altogether, how many cars were counted at both times?

_____ *2 marks*

(b) How many more vehicles were counted passing at Time B than Time A?

_____ *2 marks*

(c) Give a possible reason why this might be the case.

_____

_____ *1 mark*

4. The net of a solid shape is shown below:

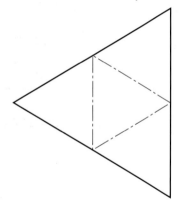

The net is made out of four equilateral triangles with sides 5 cm long.

(a) Calculate the perimeter of the net.

_____ cm   *2 marks*

(b) Circle the name of the solid shape that the net will form.

Cube   Cuboid   Prism   Pyramid   *1 mark*

(c) How many edges does the solid shape have?

_____ *1 mark*

Total Score [ ]

5. Jack's mum pays her electricity bill four times a year (quarterly). Here are her bills for one year:

| £123 | £207 | £86 | £54 |

(a) How much did she pay for her electricity over the year?

£ _____   *1 mark*

(b) If she paid directly from her bank every month, she would have saved 10% over the year. How much would she have paid each month? Show your working out.

£ _____   *3 marks*

6. The table shows how much it costs to visit a theme park.

Nasreen is 15 years old and her friend is 17 years old. Frances is 13 years old. Mum is 40 years old and Gran is 65 years old.

	Weekdays	Saturday & Sunday
Adult (15 or over)	£12	£16
Child	£6	£8
Senior Citizen	£5	£5

(a) How much will it cost Nasreen and her friend to visit on a Wednesday?

£ _____   *1 mark*

How much do they save by not going on a Saturday?

£ _____   *1 mark*

(b) Frances, Mum and Gran visit on Sunday.
How much more does it cost than if they had visited during the week?

£ _____   *2 marks*

Total Score [ ]

7. Zoe has just bought a new mobile phone. The cost of calls are shown in the table:

All calls are rounded to the nearest minute.

TIME	Cost per minute
First minute	20p
Second minute	15p
After second minute	12p

How much does Zoe pay for the following calls?

(a)   45 seconds
_____   *1 mark*

(b)   1 minute 50 seconds
_____   *2 marks*

(c)   18 minutes 20 seconds
_____   *3 marks*

8. Charlotte takes the outside temperature over two weeks at school. The results are:

WEEK 1	−2°C	0°C	2°C	3°C	0°C
WEEK 2	−6°C	2°C	1°C	−3°C	−3°C

(a)   What is the range over the two weeks?

_____ °C   *1 mark*

(b)   What is the mean average temperature:

For WEEK 1?

_____ °C   *2 marks*

For WEEK 2?

_____ °C   *2 marks*

(c)   Which week would you describe as the coldest of the two? Give a reason for your answer.

_____

_____   *2 marks*

Total Score [ ]

9. The grid has centimetre squares.

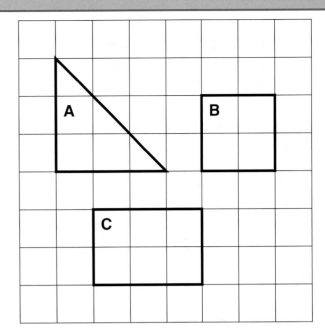

Complete the table below
which describes properties
of the 3 shapes A, B and C.

SHAPE	Number of Right Angles	Area in cm²	Lines of Symmetry
A			
B	4		
C		6	2

6 marks

10. Sam has 2 bags of coloured mints.

Bag A   Bag B

BAG A contains 24 red and 8 blue mints.
BAG B contains $\frac{1}{4}$ as many mints as BAG A.
BAG B contains all blue mints.

(a) How many mints are there altogether in BAG A?

_____ *1 mark*

How many mints are there altogether in both bags?

_____ *2 marks*

(b) What is the probability of picking a blue mint at random from BAG A?

_____ *2 marks*

(c) What is the probability of picking a red mint from BAG B?

_____ *1 mark*

Total Score [ ]

maximum 12 marks

11. $\frac{1}{5}$ of the diagram is shaded.

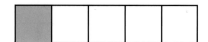

40% of the diagram is shaded.

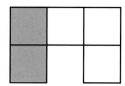

(a) Shade in 60% of the diagram below.

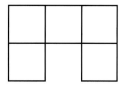

1 mark

(b) Fill in the missing number to make the fraction correct:

$40\% = \dfrac{\boxed{}}{5}$

1 mark

(c) Fill in the missing number to make the fraction correct:

$30\% = \frac{1}{5} + \dfrac{1}{\boxed{}}$

2 marks

12. Tracey thinks of a number and calls it n.
Andrew thinks of a different number and calls it x.
Tracey takes 5 away from her number.
She is left with 20.
This can be written as an equation shown below:
$n - 5 = 20$

(a) What number did Tracey think of?

_____

1 mark

(b) Write down an equation which shows how Andrew adds 15 to his number to make 20.

_____

1 mark

(c) Explain why the equation $5x = n$ is true.

_____

_____

2 marks

Total Score [ ]

13. The quadrilateral ABCD is split into two triangles.

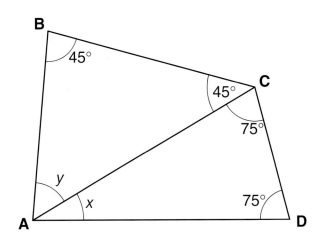

Not drawn to scale

(a) One triangle is ABC.
   Name the letters of the second triangle.

   _____ *1 mark*

(b) What kind of triangle is the second triangle?

   _____ *1 mark*

(c) Calculate angle *x*. Show your working.

   x = _____° *2 marks*

(d) Calculate angle *y*. Show your working.

   y = _____° *2 marks*

(e) Without adding all the angles together, say why angle A + angle B + angle C + angle D must make 360°.

   _____

   _____ *1 mark*

14. (a) The rectangle shown below is split into two triangles A and B.

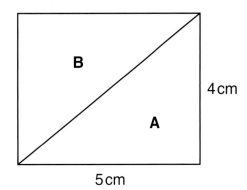

What is the area of the rectangle?

_____ cm²   *1 mark*

What is the area of triangle A?

_____ cm²   *1 mark*

(b) The rectangle shown below is *x* cm long and *y* cm wide.

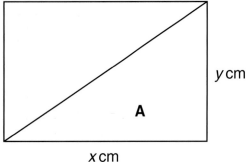

Write down an expression using the letters *x* and *y* to show the area of the rectangle.

Area of Rectangle = _____ cm²   *1 mark*

Write down an expression to show the area of triangle A.

Area of Triangle A = _____ cm²   *1 mark*

Write down an expression to show the perimeter of the rectangle.

Perimeter of Rectangle = _____ cm   *2 marks*

15. This is shape A.

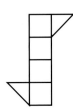

Look at the shapes shown below:

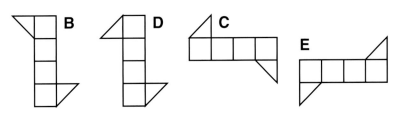

Which shapes are:

(a)   A reflection of shape A?   _____   *1 mark*

A rotation of shape A?   _____   *1 mark*

(b)   Rotate this shape 90° clockwise about the point X (2, 2). Draw the shape in its new position.

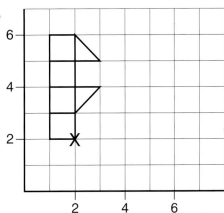

2 marks

16. Here are four number cards.

Use the correct cards to complete the following:

(a)   ☐ + ☐ = 1.3   *2 marks*

(b)   ☐ × ☐ = 0.4   *2 marks*

(c)   Which 3 cards when multiplied together give an answer closest to 0.05?

☐ × ☐ × ☐   *3 marks*

Total Score ☐

Paper 2   maximum 11 marks

29

17. Julie makes two spinners, Spinner A and Spinner B.

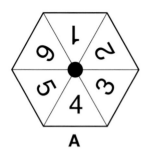

A

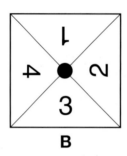

B

(a) Which spinner has more chance of showing a 1?

_____ *1 mark*

What is the probability of landing an even number on either spinner?

_____ *1 mark*

Julie tests the spinners and the results are shown in the tally charts below.

	A	B
1								
2	⟍⟋⟍⟋|	⟍⟋⟍⟋|
3						
4	||	⟍⟋⟍⟋| ||
5	⟍⟋⟍⟋|	
6	⟍⟋⟍⟋			

(b) How many times did she spin the spinners altogether?

_____ *2 marks*

Julie thinks that one spinner is biased.
Explain why Julie might be wrong.

_____

_____ *2 marks*

Total Score ☐

Tier 4-6

Paper 1: Calculator **not** allowed

Paper 2: Calculator allowed

Remember

- Each test is 1 hour long.

- You **must not** use a calculator for any question in Paper 1.

- You may use a calculator for any question in Paper 2.

- You will need: pen, pencil, rubber, ruler, protractor, a pair of compasses, tracing paper and mirror (optional).

- Each test starts with easier questions.

- Try to answer all the questions.

- Write your answers and working on the test paper – do not use any rough paper. Marks may be awarded for working.

- Check your work carefully.

- Ask your teacher if you are not sure what to do.

1. Below is the grid of a map:

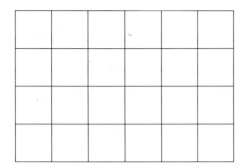

It can be split into 3 areas that make up a town on the map.

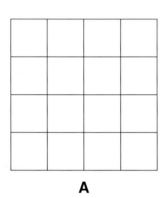 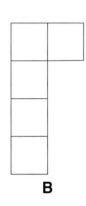 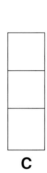

           A   **B**   **C**

(a) Which area is $\frac{1}{8}$ of the grid?   _____   *1 mark*

(b) What fraction of the grid do areas
     B and C make up when
     put together?   _____   *2 marks*

2. Jasmine and Kumar each hold a die.

(a)   Jasmine throws the die. What is the probability that the die lands on an even number?

_____   *1 mark*

(b)   They decide to add the scores on the dice.

How many ways can they make a total score of 7?
Show your working out by giving the different ways.

_____   *2 marks*

Which total scores have the lowest chance of being thrown?

_____   *2 marks*

3. 5 people queue for a roller coaster ride.
Their ages are shown below:

   18 years   12 years   26 years   10 years   34 years

(a)   What is the age range of the 5 people?

_____ years   *1 mark*

(b)   What is the mean age? Show your working out.

_____ years   *2 marks*

(c)   A sixth person joins the queue and the mean age rises to 22 years.
How old is the sixth person? Show your working out.

_____ years   *2 marks*

Total Score [ ]

4. Each square is 1 cm².

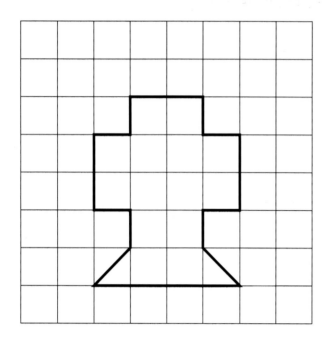

(a)   What is the area of this shape?

_____ cm²   *1 mark*

(b)   Draw its line of symmetry.   *1 mark*

(c)   Draw a rectangle around it with a perimeter of 26 cm.   *2 marks*

5. Adam's father is 48 years old and his brother Graham is half his father's age.
How old will Graham be when Adam's father is 60?
Show your working out.

_____   *3 marks*

6. Show your working out when solving the following.
Find the value of:

(a) *B*, when *N* = 40 and *G* = 25
$N = G + B$

B = _____   *2 marks*

(b) *T* when *R* = 10 and *C* = 20
$R = T \div C$

T = _____   *2 marks*

(c) *A* when *T* = 3 and *R* = 5
$2(T + R)^2 = A$

A = _____   *2 marks*

Total Score ☐

7. (a) What is the volume of the cuboid shown below?
Show your working out.

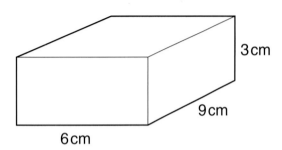

_____ cm³   *2 marks*

(b) What is the surface area of the cuboid?
Show your working out.

_____ cm²   *2 marks*

(c) If the cuboid is a container, how many 3 cm cubes would fit inside it?
Show your working out.

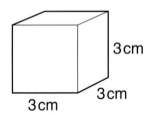

_____   *1 mark*

Total Score ☐

8. **(a)** Give the value of these squares:

3^2 = _____ 6^2 = _____ 13^2 = _____ *3 marks*

(b) Give the value of these square roots:

$\sqrt{49}$ = _____ $\sqrt{64}$ = _____ $\sqrt{225}$ = _____ *3 marks*

9. **(a)** Use compasses to construct a triangle with sides 7 cm, 6 cm and 5 cm. One side has been drawn for you.

7 cm

2 marks

(b) Measure each angle of the triangle and label them in your drawing. *3 marks*

Total Score

maximum 11 marks

10. Jack has the following coins in his right pocket:

(20p) (10p) (10p) (2p) (50p)

(a) Which extra 3 coins would he need to make £1?

_____   *2 marks*

(b) In his left pocket, he has half the value of the coins in his right.
What is the smallest number of coins that he can have in his
left pocket?
Write their values below.

_____   *2 marks*

11. The shaded pattern has one line of symmetry.

(a) What is the order of rotation for the pattern?

_____   *1 mark*

(b) Shade in 4 more squares to create a pattern which has four
lines of symmetry.   *2 marks*

Draw the other 3 lines of symmetry.   *2 marks*

What is the order of rotation for this pattern?

_____   *1 mark*

Total Score ☐

12. Simplify these expressions:

(a) $2p + 4r + 5p - 3r =$ _____   *2 marks*

(b) $(m \times m) + (n \times n) =$ _____   *2 marks*

(c) $3t + 5a - 2t - 4a + y =$ _____   *2 marks*

13. Write the following as equivalent fractions, decimals or percentages:

(a) $\frac{1}{5} = \boxed{} \%$ *1 mark*

(b) $\frac{3}{5} = \dfrac{\boxed{}}{10}$ *1 mark*

(c) $0.75 = \boxed{} \%$ *1 mark*

(d) $\frac{15}{20} = \dfrac{\boxed{}}{4}$ *1 mark*

Total Score $\boxed{}$

maximum 10 marks

14. Square B is a reflection of Square A in the *y*-axis.

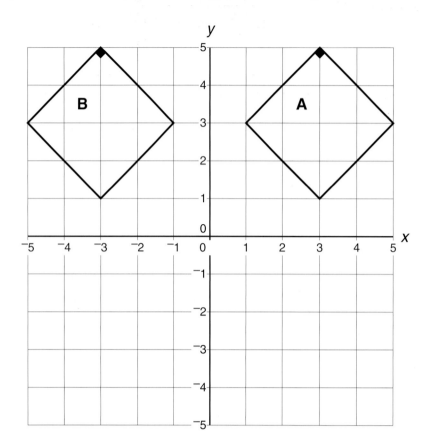

The marked corner of A has the coordinates (3, 5).

(a) What are the coordinates of the marked corner in Square B?

(_____ , _____)

2 marks

(b) Draw a third square C, which is a reflection of square A in the *x*-axis.

2 marks

(c) What are the coordinates of the marked corner in Square C?

(_____ , _____)

2 marks

Total Score

maximum 6 marks

15. A family's weekly grocery bills are shown for the month of May:

	MAY
Week 1	£80
Week 2	£100
Week 3	£120
Week 4	£60

(a)   What is the total grocery bill for the month?

£ _____   *2 marks*

What is the mean weekly bill for May?

£ _____   *2 marks*

The bills for 2 weeks in June are shown here:
The mean for the 4 weeks in June is £95 and an equal amount is spent in Week 3 and Week 4.

	JUNE
Week 1	£60
Week 2	£120

(b)   What is the total monthly bill for June?

£ _____   *1 mark*

How much is spent in Week 3 in June?

£ _____   *2 marks*

16. Rashid asked 30 pupils which subject they liked best.

SUBJECT	Number of Boys	Number of Girls
Maths	4	5
Science	3	1
English	1	9
French	0	1
Music	2	4
TOTAL	10	20

(a)   Which subject did 20% of the boys choose? _____   *2 marks*

(b)   Which subject did 45% of the girls choose? _____   *2 marks*

(c)   Which subject had a combined % popularity of 20% for the whole group of pupils?

_____   *2 marks*

Total Score [   ]

17. A student bus pass costs £45 per term.
A daily return bus ticket costs 80p.
The term lasts for 15 weeks.

    (a)   How much will a student save over one term by using a bus pass rather than paying daily?
Show your working out.

           £ _____   *2 marks*

    (b)   What is this saving as a percentage of the total return fare cost?
Show your working out.

           _____   *2 marks*

18. Solve the following equations.
Show your working out.

    (a) $3m + 2 = 17$

           $m = $ _____   *1 mark*

    (b) $4a - 3 = 2a + 5$

           $a = $ _____   *2 marks*

    (c) $5(2s - 3) = 25$

           $s = $ _____   *2 marks*

Total Score

1. $\frac{1}{5}$ of the diagram is shaded.　　　　　　　40% of the diagram is shaded.

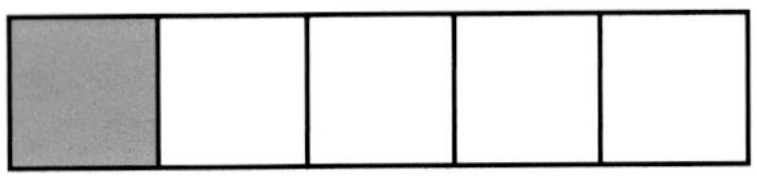

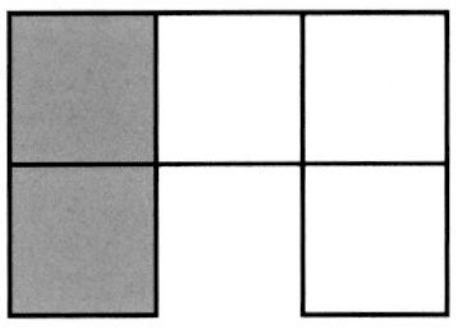

(a)　Shade in 60% of the diagram below.

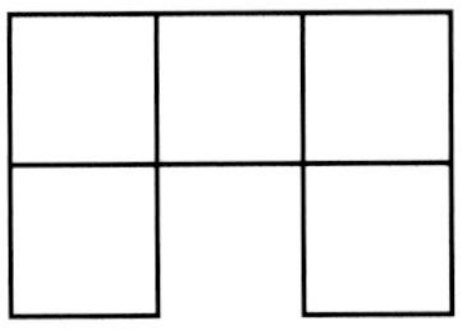

1 mark

(b)　Fill in the missing number to make the fraction correct:

$$40\% = \frac{\boxed{}}{5}$$

1 mark

(c)　Fill in the missing number to make the fraction correct:

$$30\% = \frac{1}{5} + \frac{1}{\boxed{}}$$

2 marks

2. Tracey thinks of a number and calls it n.
Andrew thinks of a different number and calls it x.
Tracey takes 5 away from her number.
She is left with 20.
This can be written as an equation shown below:
$n - 5 = 20$

(a)　What number did Tracey think of?

_____　　*1 mark*

(b)　Write down an equation which shows how Andrew adds 15 to his number to make 20.

_____　　*1 mark*

(c)　Explain why the equation $5x = n$ is true.

_____

_____　　*2 marks*

Total Score ☐

Paper 2　　　　　　　maximum 8 marks

43

3. The quadrilateral ABCD is split into two triangles.

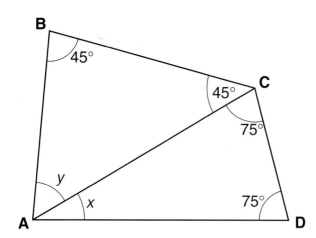

Not drawn
to scale

(a) One triangle is ABC.
Name the letters of the second triangle.

_____   *1 mark*

(b) What kind of triangle is the second triangle?

_____   *1 mark*

(c) Calculate angle *x*. Show your working.

x = _____°   *2 marks*

(d) Calculate angle *y*. Show your working.

y = _____°   *2 marks*

(e) Without adding all the angles together, say why angle A +
angle B + angle C + angle D must make 360°.

_____

_____   *1 mark*

4. (a) The rectangle shown below is split into two triangles A and B.

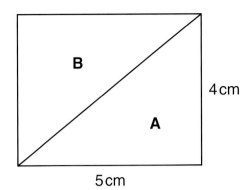

What is the area of the rectangle?

_____ cm²   *1 mark*

What is the area of triangle A?

_____ cm²   *1 mark*

(b) The rectangle shown below is *x* cm long and *y* cm wide.

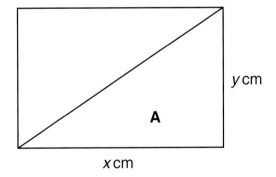

Write down an expression using the letters *x* and *y* to show the area of the rectangle.

Area of Rectangle = _____ cm²   *1 mark*

Write down an expression to show the area of triangle A.

Area of Triangle A = _____ cm²   *1 mark*

Write down an expression to show the perimeter of the rectangle.

Perimeter of Rectangle = _____ cm   *2 marks*

Total Score ☐

5. This is shape A.

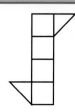

Look at the shapes shown below:

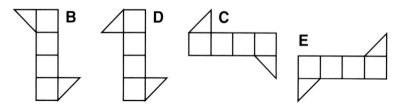

Which shapes are:

(a) A reflection of shape A? _____ *1 mark*

A rotation of shape A? _____ *1 mark*

(b) Rotate this shape 90° clockwise about the point X (2, 2). Draw the shape in its new position.

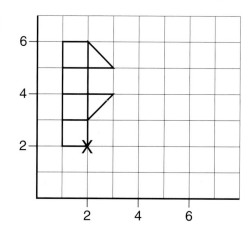

2 marks

6. Here are four number cards.

| 0.5 | 0.1 | 0.8 | 1.0 |

Use the correct cards to complete the following:

(a) ☐ + ☐ = 1.3 *2 marks*

(b) ☐ × ☐ = 0.4 *2 marks*

(c) Which 3 cards when multiplied together give an answer closest to 0.05?

☐ × ☐ × ☐ *3 marks*

7. Julie makes two spinners, Spinner A and Spinner B.

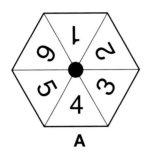

A

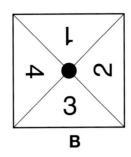

B

(a)   Which spinner has more chance of showing a 1?

_____   *1 mark*

What is the probability of landing an even number on either spinner?

_____   *1 mark*

Julie tests the spinners and the results are shown in the tally charts below.

	A	B
1								
2	⊬⊬	⊬⊬
3						
4	||	⊬⊬ ||
5	⊬⊬	
6	⊬⊬		

(b)   How many times did she spin the spinners altogether?

_____   *2 marks*

Julie thinks that one spinner is biased.
Explain why Julie might be wrong.

_____

_____   *2 marks*

Total Score

maximum 6 marks

8. (a) The grids are centimetre squares.
The square shown has a perimeter of 20 cm.

What is the area of the square?

_____ cm²   *1 mark*

(b) Draw a rectangle on the grid below which has the same perimeter as the square above.

2 marks

What is the area of the rectangle that you have drawn?

_____ cm²   *1 mark*

(c) Another rectangle can be drawn on the grid with the same perimeter but which has a different area.
Without drawing the rectangle, write down its length, width and area.

Length = _____ cm   *1 mark*

Width = _____ cm   *1 mark*

Area = _____ cm²   *1 mark*

Total Score

9. **(a)** A triangle has the angles shown.

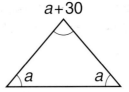

The sum of the angles can be written as the expression:
$a + a + a + 30$

Write the expression in a simpler way. _____   *1 mark*

What is the value of angle a?

$a =$ _____   *2 marks*

(b) A rectangle has the measurements shown here:

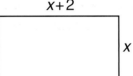

The perimeter can be written as the expression:
$2(x + 2) + 2x$

Write the expression in a simpler way. _____   *2 marks*

What is the perimeter of the rectangle if $x = 6$ cm?

Perimeter = _____ cm   *2 marks*

10. Year 8 are visiting a local factory.
$\frac{3}{4}$ of the pupils prefer the workshop to the office.
$12\frac{1}{2}$ % say they would like to work in the factory.
24 pupils prefer the office to the workshop.

(a) How many Year 8 pupils visit the factory?

_____   *2 marks*

How many pupils say they would like to work at the factory?

_____   *2 marks*

(b) $33\frac{1}{3}$ % of the pupils who prefer the office travel to school by bus.
How many pupils who prefer the office do not travel by bus?

_____   *2 marks*

Total Score

11. 9J surveyed hair and eye colours of pupils in their class. 20 pupils are girls.

Eye Colour	Number
Blue	8
Green	5
Brown	16
Other	1

Hair Colour	Number
Brown	20
Blonde	6
Red	3
Other	1

(a)   How many pupils are in class 9J?

_____   *1 mark*

(b)   If a pupil is chosen at random from the class, what is the probability that he/she will have:

Green eyes?   _____   *1 mark*

Brown hair?   _____   *1 mark*

(c)   Zoe guesses that most of the brown-haired pupils are boys. Give a reason why you think that Zoe may be wrong.

_____

_____   *1 mark*

Using the information given, estimate the number of boys with brown hair.

_____   *2 marks*

12. A supermarket sells 3 brands of lemonade. Each comes in a different size container.

2 litres 50p — A

1 litre 35p — B

750 ml 30p — C

(a)   Which brand is the cheapest per litre?

_____   *1 mark*

(b)   The cost of Brand A rises by 10% and Brand B falls by 20%. Which of the 3 brands is now the cheapest per litre?

_____   *2 marks*

Which brand is now the most expensive per litre?

_____   *2 marks*

Give a reason why people may still wish to buy this brand.

_____

_____   *2 marks*

Total Score ☐

maximum 13 marks

13. A packaging company makes cardboard gift boxes. The net of Box A is shown below. It folds to make a cuboid.

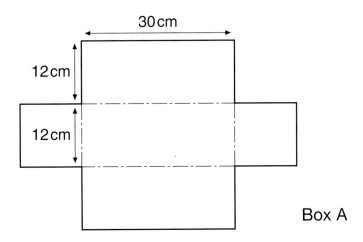

Box A

(a) How much card is used to make one box?

_____ cm²   *2 marks*

If card costs 0.2p per cm² how much does it cost the company to make 100 boxes?

£ _____   *2 marks*

(b) The company also makes Box B with measurements shown below. The box is a cube.

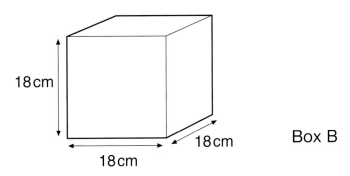

Box B

Which box (Box A or Box B) has the biggest volume? Show your working out.

_____   *3 marks*

Total Score

14. Sam is making a spinner for a game. He draws a circle with radius 5 cm and then a series of triangles each with one point at the centre. Two of the triangles are shown here:

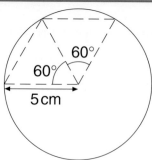

5 cm

(a) How many more triangles will Sam draw to complete the spinner?

_____ *1 mark*

(b) What is the name of the regular polygon that the triangles join to make?

_____ *1 mark*

(c) Explain why each triangle is equilateral.
Show your calculations.

_____

_____ *2 marks*

(d) Sam cuts out the polygon to make his spinner.
Calculate the perimeter of the spinner.

_____ cm   *2 marks*

15. Use as many of the following words as possible to help describe the two shapes A and B.

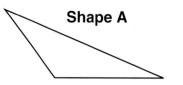

Shape A   Shape B

Parallel	Sides	Acute	Triangle
Pentagon	Equal	Straight	Obtuse
Right angle	Hexagon	Scalene	

(a) Describe Shape A: _____

_____ *3 marks*

(b) Describe Shape B: _____

_____ *3 marks*

Total Score [ ]

Tier 5-7

Paper 1: Calculator **not** allowed

Paper 2: Calculator allowed

Remember

- Each test is 1 hour long.

- You **must not** use a calculator for any question in Paper 1.

- You may use a calculator for any question in Paper 2.

- You will need: pen, pencil, rubber, ruler, protractor, a pair of compasses, tracing paper and mirror (optional).

- Each test starts with easier questions.

- Try to answer all the questions.

- Write your answers and working on the test paper – do not use any rough paper. Marks may be awarded for working.

- Check your work carefully.

- Ask your teacher if you are not sure what to do.

1. Jack has the following coins in his right pocket:

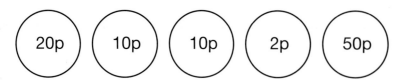

    (a) Which extra 3 coins would he need to make £1?

    _____ *2 marks*

    (b) In his left pocket, he has half the value of the coins in his right. What is the smallest number of coins that he can have in his left pocket?
Write their values below.

    _____ *2 marks*

2. The shaded pattern has one line of symmetry.

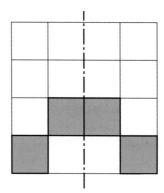

    (a) What is the order of rotation for the pattern?

                   _____ *1 mark*

    (b) Shade in 4 more squares to create a pattern which has four lines of symmetry. *2 marks*

        Draw the other 3 lines of symmetry. *2 marks*

        What is the order of rotation for this pattern?

                   _____ *1 mark*

Total Score [ ]

3. Simplify these expressions:

    (a) $2p + 4r + 5p - 3r =$ _____   *1 mark*

    (b) $(m \times m) + (n \times n) =$ _____   *2 marks*

    (c) $3t + 5a - 2t - 4a + y =$ _____   *2 marks*

4. Write the following as equivalent fractions, decimals or percentages:

    (a) $\frac{1}{5} = \boxed{} \%$ *1 mark*

    (b) $\frac{3}{5} = \dfrac{\boxed{}}{10}$ *1 mark*

    (c) $0.75 = \boxed{} \%$ *1 mark*

    (d) $\frac{15}{20} = \dfrac{\boxed{}}{4}$ *1 mark*

Total Score $\boxed{}$

Paper 1   maximum 9 marks

5. Square B is a reflection of Square A in the *y*-axis.

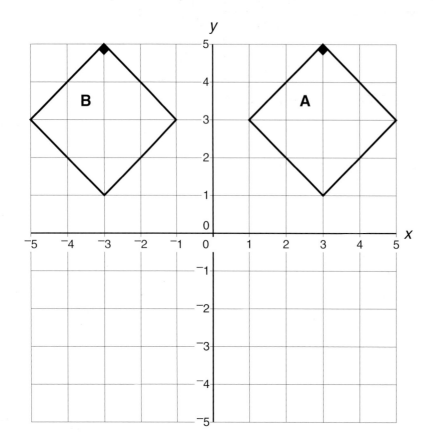

The marked corner of A has the coordinates (3, 5).

(a) What are the coordinates of the marked corner in Square B?

(_____ , _____)   *2 marks*

(b) Draw a third square C, which is a reflection of square A in the *x*-axis.

2 marks

(c) What are the coordinates of the marked corner in Square C?

(_____ , _____)   *2 marks*

Total Score

maximum 6 marks

6. A family's weekly grocery bills are shown for the month of May:

	MAY
Week 1	£80
Week 2	£100
Week 3	£120
Week 4	£60

(a)   What is the total grocery bill for the month?

£ _____   *2 marks*

What is the mean weekly bill for May?

£ _____   *2 marks*

The bills for 2 weeks in June are shown here:
The mean for the 4 weeks in June is £95 and an equal amount is spent in Week 3 and Week 4.

	JUNE
Week 1	£60
Week 2	£120

(b)   What is the total monthly bill for June?

£ _____   *1 mark*

How much is spent in Week 3 in June?

£ _____   *2 marks*

7. Rashid asked 30 pupils which subject they liked best.

SUBJECT	Number of Boys	Number of Girls
Maths	4	5
Science	3	1
English	1	9
French	0	1
Music	2	4
TOTAL	10	20

(a)   Which subject did 20% of the boys choose? _____   *2 marks*

(b)   Which subject did 45% of the girls choose? _____   *2 marks*

(c)   Which subject had a combined % popularity of 20% for the whole group of pupils?

_____   *2 marks*

Total Score [ ]

8. A student bus pass costs £45 per term.
A daily return bus ticket costs 80p.
The term lasts for 15 weeks.

(a)   How much will a student save over one term by using a bus
pass rather than paying daily?
Show your working out.

£ _____   *2 marks*

(b)   What is this saving as a percentage of the total return fare cost?
Show your working out.

_____   *2 marks*

9. Solve the following equations.
Show your working out.

(a) $3m + 2 = 17$

$m = $ _____   *1 mark*

(b) $4a - 3 = 2a + 5$

$a = $ _____   *1 mark*

(c) $5(2s - 3) = 25$

$s = $ _____   *2 marks*

10. The grid below is marked in rectangles.
Each rectangle is '*a*' wide and '*b*' long. The diagonal distance is '*c*'.
Three shapes: S, T and V are shown on the grid.

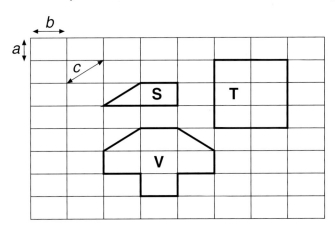

The perimeter of shape S is given by the expression: $a + 3b + c$

(a) Write down the perimeters of shapes T and V in their simplest form.
Show your working out.

Perimeter of shape T: _____ *1 mark*

Perimeter of shape V: _____ *1 mark*

(b) Work out the area of Shape T.
Write it in its simplest form.

Area of shape T: _____ *2 marks*

11. The following number line is marked in tenths.

$$0 \qquad\qquad\qquad \tfrac{1}{2} \qquad\qquad\qquad 1$$

(a) Mark with an arrow where $\frac{3}{5}$ lies. *1 mark*

(b) Subtract $\frac{3}{10}$ from $\frac{3}{5}$.

_____ *1 mark*

(c) $1\frac{3}{4} + \frac{5}{8} =$ _____ *2 marks*

Total Score [ ]

maximum 8 marks

12. Below are five number cards:

| 0.2 | $\frac{1}{4}$ | 30% | 0.5 | $1\frac{4}{5}$ |

Use the cards to complete the following:

(a) ☐ + ☐ = 0.7 *1 mark*

(b) ☐ x 100 = 20 *1 mark*

(c) ☐ + ☐ = $\frac{3}{4}$ *1 marks*

(d) 2 – ☐ = $\frac{1}{5}$ *1 mark*

13. The diagram shows a triangle ABC drawn on a square grid.

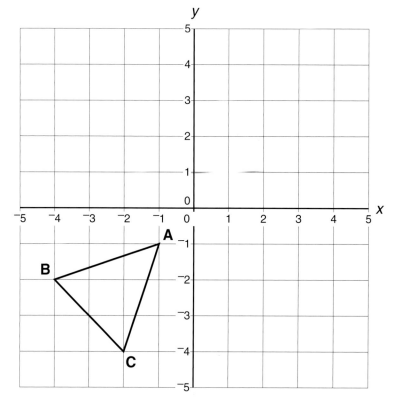

(a) On the grid, draw the line $y = -x$. *1 mark*

(b) Write down the coordinates of the vertices A, B and C.

A = (,) B = (,) C = (,) *3 marks*

(c) Draw the reflection of ABC in the line $y = -x$ and label the triangle DEF. *2 marks*

Write down the coordinates of DEF.

D = (,) E = (,) F = (,) *3 marks*

Total Score ☐

14. Michael has the following coins in his pockets:

Right pocket: 20p, 2p, 5p, 10p

Left pocket: 50p, 10p, 10p

(a)   If he takes one coin out of either pocket, what is the chance of him choosing:

20p   _____   *1 mark*

10p   _____   *1 mark*

£1   _____   *1 mark*

(b)   If Michael takes one coin from each pocket, what is the chance of choosing coins with a total value of more than 20p?
Show your working out.

_____   *2 marks*

Total Score

15. (a) Draw arrows to join the equivalent equations:

$x + y = 3$ $2x + 6 = 8y$

$x = 4y - 3$ $2x^2 + 12 = 6y$

$3x + 6y = 9$ $4x = 12 - 4y$

$x^2 = 3y - 6$ $3(x + 2y) - 9 = 0$ *3 marks*

(b) Solve the following inequalities:

$5t + 10 \leq 15$

_____   *2 marks*

$\frac{a}{5} - 1 > 6$

_____   *2 marks*

Total Score [ ]

16. A rectangular school yard is split into zones, R, T and V as shown.
The length and width of the playground are shown on the diagram.

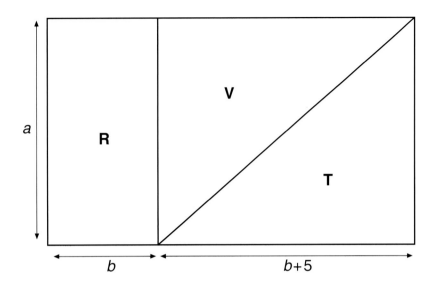

(a) What is the area of zone R?

_____ *1 mark*

What is the area of zone T in terms of *a* and *b*?
Write the expression in its simplest form.

_____ *2 marks*

(b) The width of the playground is 20 m.
If the area of zone T is 140 m², find:

The value of *b*.

b = _____ *2 marks*

The area of the playground in square metres.

Area of playground = _____ m²   *2 marks*

17. (a) Enlarge the shape ABCDEF by a scale factor of 2, centre (0, 0).

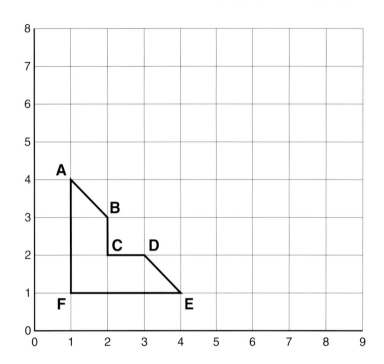

2 marks

(b) Enlarge the shape ABC by a scale factor of $\frac{1}{2}$, centre (0, 0).

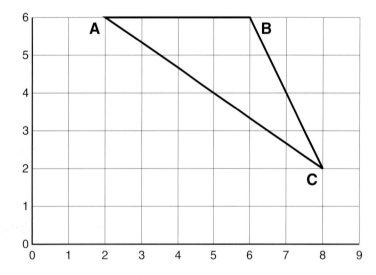

2 marks

Total Score

maximum 4 marks

1. (a) The grids are centimetre squares.
The square shown has a perimeter of 20 cm.

What is the area of the square?

_____ cm² *1 mark*

(b) Draw a rectangle on the grid below which has the same perimeter as the square above.

1 mark

What is the area of the rectangle that you have drawn?

_____ cm² *1 mark*

(c) Another rectangle can be drawn on the grid with the same perimeter but which has a different area.
Without drawing the rectangle, write down its length, width and area.

Length = _____ cm *1 mark*

Width = _____ cm *1 mark*

Area = _____ cm² *1 mark*

Total Score ☐

2. **(a)** A triangle has the angles shown.

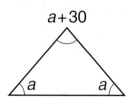

The sum of the angles can be written as the expression:
$a + a + a + 30$

Write the expression in a simpler way. _____   *1 mark*

What is the value of angle a?

$a =$ _____   *2 marks*

(b) A rectangle has the measurements shown below:

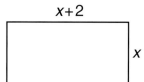

The perimeter can be written as the expression:
$2(x + 2) + 2x$

Write the expression in a simpler way. _____   *2 marks*

What is the perimeter of the rectangle if $x = 6$ cm?

Perimeter = _____ cm   *1 mark*

3. Year 8 are visiting a local factory.
$\frac{3}{4}$ of the pupils prefer the workshop to the office.
$12\frac{1}{2}$ % say they would like to work in the factory.
24 pupils prefer the office to the workshop.

(a) How many Year 8 pupils visit the factory?

_____   *2 marks*

How many pupils say they would like to work at the factory?

_____   *1 mark*

(b) $33\frac{1}{3}$ % of the pupils who prefer the office travel to school by bus.
How many pupils who prefer the office do not travel by bus?

_____   *2 marks*

Total Score

4. 9J surveyed hair and eye colours of pupils in their class. 20 pupils are girls.

Eye Colour	Number		Hair Colour	Number
Blue	8		Brown	20
Green	5		Blonde	6
Brown	16		Red	3
Other	1		Other	1

(a) How many pupils are in class 9J?

_____   *1 mark*

(b) If a pupil is chosen at random from the class, what is the probability that he/she will have:

Green eyes?   _____   *1 mark*

Brown hair?   _____   *1 mark*

(c) Zoe guesses that most of the brown-haired pupils are boys. Give a reason why you think that Zoe may be wrong.

_____

_____   *1 mark*

Using the information given, estimate the number of boys with brown hair.

_____   *2 marks*

5. A supermarket sells 3 brands of lemonade. Each comes in a different size container.

(a) Which brand is the cheapest per litre?

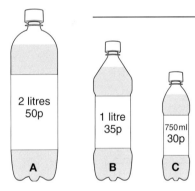

2 litres
50p

A

1 litre
35p

B

750 ml
30p

C

_____   *1 mark*

(b) The cost of Brand A rises by 10% and Brand B falls by 20%. Which of the 3 brands is now the cheapest per litre?

_____   *2 marks*

Which brand is now the most expensive per litre?

_____   *2 marks*

Give a reason why people may still wish to buy this brand.

_____

_____   *1 mark*

Total Score

maximum 12 marks

6. A packaging company makes cardboard gift boxes. The net of Box A is shown below. It folds to make a cuboid.

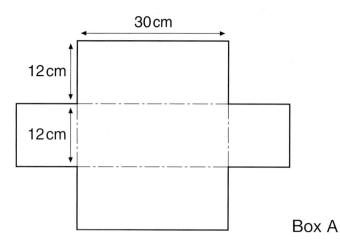

Box A

(a)   How much card is used to make one box?

_____ cm²   *2 marks*

If card costs 0.2p per cm² how much does it cost the company to make 100 boxes?

£ _____   *2 marks*

(b)   The company also makes Box B with measurements shown below. The box is a cube.

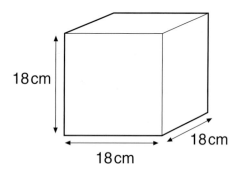

Box B

Which box (Box A or Box B) has the biggest volume?
Show your working out.

_____   *2 marks*

Total Score

7. Sam is making a spinner for a game.
He draws a circle with radius 5 cm
and then a series of triangles each with
one point at the centre. Two of the
triangles are shown here:

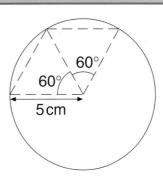

5 cm

(a) How many more triangles will Sam draw to complete the spinner?

_____ *1 mark*

(b) What is the name of the regular polygon that the triangles join
to make?

_____ *1 mark*

(c) Explain why each triangle is equilateral.
Show your calculations.

_____

_____ *2 marks*

(d) Sam cuts out the polygon to make his spinner.
Calculate the perimeter of the spinner.

_____ cm *1 mark*

8. Use as many of the following words as possible to help describe
the two shapes A and B.

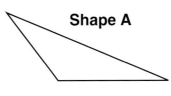

Shape A   **Shape B**

Parallel   Sides   Acute   Triangle
Pentagon   Equal   Straight   Obtuse
Right angle   Hexagon   Scalene

(a) Describe Shape A: _____

_____ *2 marks*

(b) Describe Shape B: _____

_____ *2 marks*

Total Score

9. A child's puzzle has 5 pieces arranged as shown on the grid to make a rectangle.

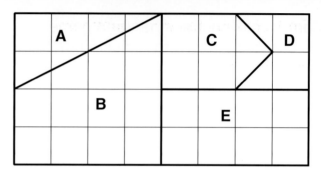

Each piece is a fraction of the whole puzzle. The fraction values of A and E are shown below:

$A = \frac{1}{8}$ $\qquad\qquad$ $E = \frac{1}{4}$

(a) Complete the fractions for the other pieces.

$B = \dfrac{\Box}{\Box}$ $\qquad$ $C = \dfrac{\Box}{\Box}$ $\qquad$ $D = \dfrac{\Box}{\Box}$ $\qquad$ *3 marks*

(b) Which piece of the puzzle has the same fraction value as piece A + piece E?

_____ *1 mark*

(c) What fraction of the whole puzzle do pieces B, E and D make together? Show your working out.

_____ *2 marks*

10. Class 8S has the ratio of girls to boys as 6:5.

(a) If there are 18 girls, how many pupils are there altogether in the class? Show your working out.

_____ *2 marks*

(b) 3 girls leave the class.
What is the new ratio of girls to boys in its simplest form?

_____ *2 marks*

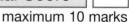

Total Score ☐

11. Find x in the following equations:

(a) $\frac{3}{4} = \frac{6}{x}$

$x =$ _____ *1 mark*

(b) $\frac{3}{4} = \frac{x}{18}$

$x =$ _____ *1 mark*

(c) $\frac{3.5}{4} = \frac{x}{10}$

$x =$ _____ *1 mark*

12. Raj is testing reaction times of pupils in his class by dropping a 30 cm ruler between two fingers. He records the point on the ruler at which it is caught. The higher the figure, the slower the reaction time. He measures 10 boys and 10 girls.

Boys (cm)	12	15	20	23	17	19	28	30	18	23
Girls (cm)	14	13	17	22	11	6	20	24	15	22

(a) What is the mean and range in reaction times:

For the boys?

Mean = _____ cm   Range = _____ cm   *3 marks*

For the girls?

Mean = _____ cm   Range = _____ cm   *3 marks*

(b) Raj concludes that boys have slower reaction times than girls. Give a reason why you might disagree with Raj's conclusion.

_____

_____   *1 mark*

Total Score ☐

maximum 10 marks

13. A factory makes CDs. They are pressed in fours from a square as shown on the diagram. The radius of each CD is length '*a*'.

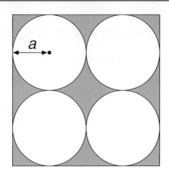

(a)   What is the length of the square in terms of *a*? _____   *1 mark*

(b)   Explain why the area of the shaded waste material is given by the expression $16a^2 - 4\pi a^2$.

_____

_____   *2 marks*

14. Kate and Frances are collecting data about fashion. They record the number of pairs of shoes owned by 20 boys in Year 9.
The graph shows the percentage of boys owning between 1 and 6 pairs of shoes.

(a)   Using the information in the graph, complete the frequency table. The first entry is done for you.

Pairs of shoes	% of boys	Number of boys
1	20%	4
2		
3		
4		
5		
6		
Total	100%	20

5 marks

(b)   What is the total number of pairs of shoes owned by all of the boys? Show your working.   _____   *2 marks*

(c)   Calculate the mean number of pairs of shoes owned by the boys.   _____   *2 marks*

Total Score ☐

15. The table below shows four number patterns.

	1	2	3	4	5	6	n
A	3	6	9	12	15	18	$3n$
B	1	5					$4n-3$
C				16	25		n^2
D	0	7	26	63	124	215	

(a)   Complete the missing values for patterns B and C and the
       missing expression for pattern D.   *3 marks*

(b)   Using the table of number patterns to help you, draw the graphs
       for the equations $y = 3x$ and $y = 4x - 3$.
       Solve the simultaneous equations from the graph.

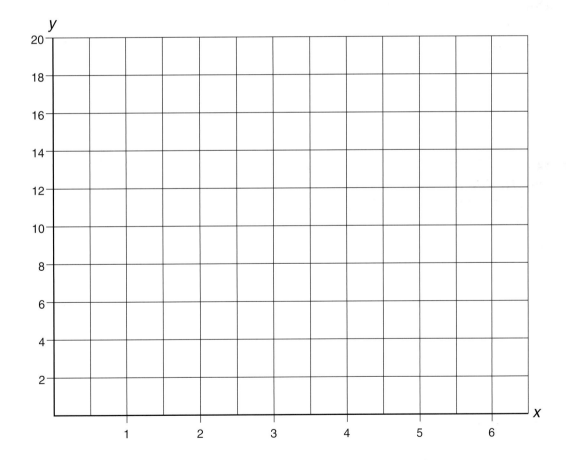

       $x =$ _____ $y =$ _____   *2 marks*

Total Score

maximum 5 marks

16. Chai takes a photograph using a digital camera. His first print has the dimensions shown here:

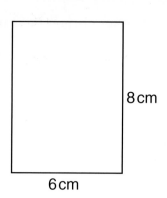

8 cm

6 cm

(a) For a second print, he reduces the print using a scale factor of 0.8. Calculate the length and width of the new print.

Length = _____ cm   Width = _____ cm   *2 marks*

(b) He wants to frame the photograph using the following measurements:

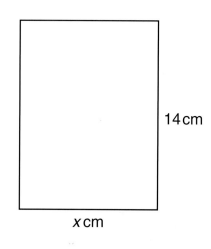

He keeps the same proportions as the original print. Calculate the value of x.

14 cm

x cm

x = _____   *2 marks*

17. (a) Solve the following inequality:

$6x - 2 < 3x + 4$

_____   *2 marks*

(b) Solve the simultaneous equations:

$2x - y = 10$
$x + 3y = 5$

x = _____ y = _____   *3 marks*

Total Score [ ]

Mental Maths Test 1

Read each question carefully, twice. Write your answers on the sheet provided on page 77.

For this group of questions you will have 5 seconds to work out each answer and write it down.

1.	What is 30% as a decimal?
2.	What is 125 multiplied by 5?
3.	My car is 2.3 metres long, how many centimetres is it?
4.	What is the sum of these two numbers: 54 and 67?
5.	Write down in digits, one million four hundred and three.
6.	Simplify the expression shown on the sheet.

For the next group of questions you will have 10 seconds to work out each answer and write it down.

7.	I am facing north. If I turn 270° anti-clockwise, what direction am I facing?
8.	The bus is due at 10.57, it is now 09.45. How long is it until it arrives?
9.	I buy three books. The first two cost £1.75 and the third costs £2.50, how much is the total cost?
10.	What fraction is 12.5 of 100?
11.	Add 4.3 to 7.4.
12.	Estimate the length of the line shown on your sheet.
13.	What is the area of the triangle shown?
14.	Solve the equation shown on the sheet.
15.	There are 3 red sweets, 5 blue sweets and 8 green sweets in a bag. What is the probability that I choose a green sweet?

16.	I blink 30 times in 1 minute. How many times do I blink in 3 hours?
17.	Multiply out the brackets: $3x(4x + 2)$.
18.	What is the mean of the five numbers shown on the sheet?
19.	What is 30 multiplied by negative 3?
20.	What is 8 cubed?

For the next group of questions you will have 15 seconds to work out each answer and write it down.

21.	Which is the smallest fraction shown on the sheet?
22.	What is 23 multiplied by 7?
23.	The ratio of boys to girls in a class is 3:4. There are 35 pupils in the class. How many are girls?
24.	What is the volume of the shape shown on the sheet?
25.	One Euro is approximately 60p sterling. How much is 200 Euros in pounds sterling?
26.	What is the square root of 36?
27.	I am travelling at 30 mph for $1\frac{1}{2}$ hours. How far do I travel?
28.	Write down three consecutive numbers that add up to 66.
29.	14 x 24 = 336. What is 3360 ÷ 14?
30.	There are four pairs of numbers shown on your sheet. Circle the pair between which the square root of 152 lies.

Mental Maths Test 2

Read each question carefully, twice. Write your answers on the sheet provided on page 78.

For this first group of questions you will have 5 seconds to work out each answer and write it down.

1.	What is 5^3?
2.	How many eights are in 72?
3.	What is 45% as a decimal?
4.	What is the sum of 144 and 265?
5.	Look at the expression shown on the sheet. Simplify it.
6.	Subtract 5 from negative 2.

For the next group of questions you will have 10 seconds to work out each answer and write it down.

7.	Look at the calculation shown on the sheet. Work out the answer.
8.	Look at the equation shown on the sheet. If R equals 5, what is H?
9.	What is 20% of £320?
10.	How many times does 0.2 go into 3?
11.	A car travelling at 100 km per hour completes its journey in y minutes. If the journey is 50 km, what is y?
12.	How many edges has a cube?
13.	The ratio of boys to girls in a class is 2:3. If there are 30 pupils in the class, how many girls are there?
14.	Write a factor of 56 that is a multiple of 4.
15.	What is the volume of the prism shown on the sheet?

16.	The pie chart shows the percentage of pupils who use different modes of travel to school. If walking is 10% and cycling is half of that, what is the percentage of people who catch the bus?
17.	What is the mean of the numbers shown on your sheet?
18.	Estimate the size of the angle shown on your sheet.
19.	The entry fee to a theme park falls from £12 to £9. What percentage reduction is this?
20.	Write an approximate answer to the calculation shown on your sheet.

For the next group of questions you will have 15 seconds to work out each answer and write it down.

21.	A 50 minute lesson ended at 1.15 pm. What time did it start?
22.	When I was 46, my son was half my age. I'm now 60 so how old is he?
23.	Look at the circle shown on your sheet. If πd is the circumference of the circle and π is approximately 3.1416, what is the circumference (to 1 decimal place)?
24.	The diagram on your sheet shows angles in a rhombus. If $x = 60$, what is y?
25.	Multiply the fractions: $\frac{3}{10} \times \frac{3}{15}$.
26.	Add together 3^3 and 5^2.
27.	The mean of two numbers is 9. One of the numbers is negative 5. What is the other number?
28.	Fill in the missing number in the number sequence.
29.	Divide 4 minutes in 8 equal parts. How many seconds in each part?
30.	Two planes fly one above the other, and the distance between them always stays the same. The planes are .... to each other.

Mental Maths Test 1 answer sheet

Ask someone to read the questions for Test 1 to you. Each question will be read twice and you will have a fixed time to complete the answer. For questions 1 to 6, it will be 5 seconds. For questions 7 to 20, it will be 10 seconds and for questions 21 to 30, it will be 15 seconds.
You only need this paper and a pencil.
Calculators are not allowed.

1.		**16.**	
2.		**17.**	
3.	cm	**18.**	10, 30, 7, 35, 13
4.		**19.**	
5.		**20.**	
6.	$y + y + y - 10$	**21.**	$\frac{1}{3}$, $\frac{1}{16}$, $\frac{2}{8}$, $\frac{3}{4}$, $\frac{4}{5}$
7.		**22.**	
8.		**23.**	
9.	£	**24.**	cm³ 2cm 10cm 8cm
10.		**25.**	£
11.		**26.**	
12.	cm	**27.**	miles
13.	cm² 4cm 7cm	**28.**	
14.	$4 = 2x + 6$	**29.**	
15.		**30.**	7, 8 4, 5 8, 9 12, 13

Total Marks

77

Mental Maths Test 2 answer sheet

Ask someone to read the questions for Test 2 to you. Each question will be read twice and you will have a fixed time to complete the answer. For questions 1 to 6, it will be 5 seconds. For questions 7 to 20, it will be 10 seconds and for questions 21 to 30, it will be 15 seconds.
You only need this paper and a pencil.
Calculators are not allowed.

1.		**16.**	
2.			
3.		**17.**	3, 7, 3, 4, 6, 1
4.		**18.**	°
5.	$4y + 2y + y - w$		
6.		**19.**	
7.	$7(4 + 6)$	**20.**	$60.1 \div 0.49$
8.	$H = \frac{4R}{2}$	**21.**	
9.	£	**22.**	
10.		**23.**	cm
11.		**24.**	
12.		**25.**	
13.		**26.**	
14.		**27.**	
15.		**28.**	5.5, 6.2, _____, 7.6
		29.	sec
		30.	

Total Marks [ ]

Answers and tips

Tier 3–5

Paper 1

1. (a)

School dinners	● ● ●
Sandwiches	● ●
No dinner	●

2 marks

  (b) 28 pupils   1 mark

Tip: Students are required to draw, use and interpret a range of diagrams at this level including line and bar graphs as well as pictograms where the symbol represents an object or a number of objects.

2. (a) 30°C   2 marks
  (b) 40°C difference   2 marks
  (c) Thermometer A   2 marks

Tip: This question is about negative numbers in the context of temperature. Students also need to know how to add, subtract, multiply and divide negative numbers for higher attainment levels.

3. (a) 9 x 4 = 36 or 4 x 9 = 36   2 marks
  (b) 10 ÷ 5 = 2 or 10 ÷ 2 = 5   3 marks
  (c) (5 + 4) x 9 = 81 or (4 + 5) x 9 = 81   3 marks

Tip: Trial and improvement at a simple level will give the correct answers here. In (c) students need to understand the effect of brackets on the order of operations.

4. (a) B = 135°, C = 45° and D = 90°   3 marks
  (b) 13.5 cm²   *1 mark for 13.5, 1 mark for cm²*   2 marks

Tip: Students are required to understand angle notation and special angles, (e.g. acute, obtuse, reflex, right angle) as well as angle properties of triangles and quadrilaterals.

5. (a) Letters A, H and T have line symmetry   2 marks
  (b)   2 marks

Tip: Line or reflective symmetry can be illustrated by using a mirror or by folding shapes along the line of symmetry. For a shape to be symmetrical, the folded shape should completely cover the other half.

6. (a) £1 – 65p = 35p change   2 marks
  (b) £1.75   2 marks
  (c) He could buy spaceships and toffee   2 marks

7. (a) 20, 40, 60, 80, 100   2 marks
  (b) 1, 1, 2, 3, 5, 8, 13   2 marks
  (c) 1, 2, 4, 8, 16, 32   2 marks

   (d)   80, 40, 20, 10, 5, 2.5   *3 marks*

Tip: This question involves number sequences. Missing numbers can usually be found by looking at the numbers either side and finding the difference. Some sequences involve special numbers such as squares, cubes, primes or triangular numbers.

8. (a)   0.047   *1 mark*
     (b)   0.047, 0.4070, 0.47, 47, 477.0   *2 marks*

Tip: Students need to appreciate the size of numbers and the importance of place value and decimal notation. The size of numbers is especially important when estimating and approximating values with or without calculators as often a calculator answer will be accepted despite the incorrect pressing of keys.

9. (a)   2   *1 mark*
     (b)   18   *1 mark*
     (c)   9   *1 mark*
     (d)   13   *1 mark*

Tip: Knowledge of number properties is a feature here with terms such as prime, multiple and factor being used. A prime number has only two factors – one and itself. Factors come in pairs and multiply together to make a product, e.g. 3 x 4 = 12. Three and four are both factors of the product 12.

10. (a) Area C   *1 mark*
     (b) $\frac{1}{3}$ of the grid   *2 marks*

11. (a) $\frac{1}{2}$ *1 mark*
     (b) 6 ways of making 7: 1 + 6, 2 + 5, 3 + 4, 4 + 3, 5 + 2, 6 + 1; *2 marks*
         1 + 1 =2 and 6 + 6 = 12   *2 marks*

Tip: The theoretical probability of a score on a die being thrown is the number of events involved divided by the total number of possible events. For an even number to be thrown, therefore, it is three (2, 4, 6) divided by six (1, 2, 3, 4, 5, 6) or one-half.

12. (a) Age range is 34 – 10 = 24 years   *1 mark*
     (b) Mean age is 100 ÷ 5 = 20 years   *2 marks*
     (c) 6 x 22 = 132, 132 – 100 = 32, sixth person is 32 years old *2 marks*

Tip: The range is the difference between the smallest and largest measure. The mean is a measure of average together with the mode (most frequent) and the median (the middle).

13. (a) Area of the shape is 15 cm²   *1 mark*
     (b)   *1 mark*

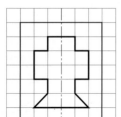

     (c) See outer rectangle in diagram in (b)   *2 marks*

14. $48 \div 2 = 24$, $60 - 48 = 12$,
in 12 years' time, Graham will be 36 years old
3 marks

> Tip: This problem needs to be broken down into stages. The three
> stages are shown above. Practice with similar problems will help the
> student to analyse what is required by the question.

15. (a) $40 = 25 + 15$, $B = 15$ *2 marks*
(b) $10 = 200 \div 20$, $T = 200$ *2 marks*
(c) $2(3 + 5)^2 = A$, $2 \times 64 = 128$, $A = 128$ *2 marks*

> Tip: This question involves simple substitution into expressions. In (c)
> remember to square the contents of the bracket before multiplying by
> two.

16. (a) $6 \times 9 \times 3 = 54 \times 3 = 162$ cm³ *2 marks*
(b) $9 \times 6) \times 2 = 108$ cm², $(6 \times 3) \times 2 = 36$ cm²,
$(9 \times 3) \times 2 = 54$ cm², Total = 198 cm² *2 marks*
(c) $2 \times 3 = 6$ cubes could fit inside *1 mark*

> Tip: Students need to know how to calculate the volume of cubes,
> cuboids and some prisms. The unit of volume is a cubic measure such
> as cm³ or m³.

17. (a) 9; 36; 169 *3 marks*
(b) 7; 8; 15 *3 marks*

18. (a) *2 marks*

(b) Angles given in diagram in (a) *3 marks*

> Tip: Allow correct answers to 1° margin less than or greater than the
> ones given above.

Total 90 Marks

Tier 3–5

Paper 2

1. (a) Right angled isosceles triangle *1 mark*
(b) *1 mark*

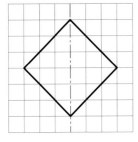

81

(c) Square   *1 mark*

> Tip: It is important that students can recognise mathematical shapes which have been rotated about the vertical axis. The shape in (c) must be named 'square' rather than the often-used but mathematically incorrect 'diamond'.

2. (a) 9 + −3 = 6   *2 marks*
   (b)   −7, −3, 0, 9   *2 marks*
   (c) 9 + −3 + −7 = −1   *3 marks*

> Tip: In (a) and (c), the numbers can be used in any order as 9 + −3 is equivalent to −3 + 9.

3. (a) 22 + 35 = 57 cars   *2 marks*
   (b) 83 − 54 = 29 more vehicles   *2 marks*
   (b) Time B could have been a rush hour period   *1 mark*

4. (a) Perimeter is 30 cm   *2 marks*
   (b) Pyramid   *1 mark*
   (c) 6 edges   *1 mark*

> Tip: This pyramid is triangular based. Students need to know about the common properties of 3-dimensional shapes including the recognition of faces, edges and vertices.

5. (a) £470   *1 mark*
   (b) 10% of £470 = £47, £470 − £47 = £423,
       £423 ÷ 12 = £35.25 each month   *3 marks*

> Tip: Payment on a monthly basis by direct debit is now encouraged by many utility companies and often results in a saving over other methods. Students will benefit from seeing actual bills and how much a household can save using this method of payment.

6. (a) 2 x £12 = £24 is cost on Wednesday;   *1 mark*
       2 x £16 = £32, £32 − £24 = £8 they save   *1 mark*
   (b) £8 + £16 + £5 = £29 cost on Sunday,
       £6 + £12 + £5 = £23 cost on weekday,
       so costs £6 more on a Sunday   *2 marks*

> Tip: Questions involving tables of information and retrieving the correct information are common. Practice can be gained from sources such as travel timetables and fare pricing.

7. (a) Cost of 1 minute = 20p   *1 mark*
   (b) Cost of 2 minutes = 20p + 15p = 35p   *2 marks*
   (c) Cost of 18 minutes = 20p + 15p + 192p = £2.27   *3 marks*

> Tip: Students need to interpret the wording carefully. For instance, in (c) it is necessary to calculate the rate at the first and then second minute before adding this to the constant rate beyond the second minute.

8. (a) 3°C − −6°C = 9°C is the range   *1 mark*
   (b) (−2 + 0 + 2 + 3 + 0) ÷ 5 = 0.6°C for Week 1   *2 marks*
       (−6 + 2 + 1 + −3 + −3) ÷ 5 = −1.8°C for Week 2   *2 marks*

(c) Week 2 has coldest day and coldest mean temperature   *2 marks*

> Tip: This question is about the range and mean of two sets of numbers including negative numbers. In order to find the range, it is necessary to recognise the difference between −6 and +3.

9. A – 1 right angle, 4.5 cm², 1 line of symmetry
   B – 4 right angles, 4 cm², 4 lines of symmetry
   C – 4 right angles, 6 cm², 2 lines of symmetry   *6 marks*

10. (a) 32 mints in Bag A;   *1 mark*
          32 + 8 = 40 mints altogether   *2 marks*
   (b) $\frac{8}{32} = \frac{1}{4}$ *2 marks*
   (c) 0   *1 mark*

> Tip: In (c), the student needs to know that there are no red mints in Bag B and that this is represented by 0 in the rules of probability where 1 is a certainty.

11. (a)   *1 mark*

   (b) 40% = $\frac{2}{5}$ *1 mark*
   (c) 30% = $\frac{1}{5} + \frac{1}{10}$ *2 marks*

> Tip: A knowledge of common fractions and percentage equivalence is required here. The student is helped by means of the shapes which are split into squares. The answer to (b) can be deduced from the shape in (a). Each square represents 20% or $\frac{1}{5}$.

12. (a) $n = 25$ *1 mark*
   (b) $x + 15 = 20$ *1 mark*
   (c) The equation is true because $n = 25$ and $x = 5$ from
        parts (a) and (b). Therefore 5 x 5 = 25.   *2 marks*

> Tip: Here, the student is required to construct simple equations from the worded problem. In (c), the answers to the other parts are required in order to obtain the correct solution.

13. (a) ACD   *1 mark*
   (b) Isosceles   *1 mark*
   (c) 80° − (75° + 75°) = 30°   *2 marks*
   (d) 180° − (80° + 45°) = 55°   *2 marks*
   (e) The sum of the angles in a quadrilateral is 360°   *1 mark*

> Tip: This question requires a knowledge of internal angles within triangles and quadrilaterals and in particular, the fact that the sum of the interior angles of a triangle is 180° and that of a quadrilateral is 360°.

14. (a) Area of rectangle is 5 x 4 = 20 cm²;   *1 mark*
        Area of triangle is (4 x 5) ÷ 2 = 10 cm²   *1 mark*
   (b) Area of rectangle = $x \times y$ or xy cm²   *1 mark*
        Area of triangle = $\frac{1}{2}xy$ cm²   *1 mark*
        Perimeter of rectangle = $2x + 2y$ *2 marks*

15. (a) Shape B is a reflection of Shape A   *1 mark*
Shape C is a rotation of Shape A   *1 mark*
(b)   *2 marks*

16. (a) 0.5 + 0.8 = 1.3 or 0.8 + 0.5 = 1.3   *2 marks*
(b) 0.5 x 0.8 = 0.4 or 0.8 x 0.5 = 0.4   *2 marks*
(c) 0.5 x 0.1 x 1.0 = 0.05   *3 marks*

17. (a) Spinner B;   *1 mark*
Probability $= \frac{1}{2}$ *1 mark*
(b) 40 times;   *2 marks*
There are not enough trials for either spinner in order for this conclusion to be made; also, Spinner A has been spun more times than B so the comparison would not be fair   *2 marks*

| **Total 90 Marks** |

Tier 4–6

Paper 1

1. (a) Area C   *1 mark*
(b) $\frac{1}{3}$ of the grid   *2 marks*

2. (a) $\frac{1}{2}$ *1 mark*
(b) 6 ways of making 7: 1 + 6, 2 + 5, 3 + 4, 4 + 3, 5 + 2, 6 + 1;   *2 marks*
1 + 1 = 2 and 6 + 6 = 12   *2 marks*

3. (a) Age range is 34 – 10 = 24 years   *1 mark*
(b) Mean age is 100 ÷ 5 = 20 years   *2 marks*
(c) 6 x 22 = 132, 132 – 100 = 32, sixth person is 32 years old   *2 marks*

Tip: The range is the difference between the smallest and largest measure. The mean is a measure of average together with the mode (most frequent) and the median (the middle).

4. (a)   (a) Area of the shape is 15 cm²   *1 mark*
    (b)   *1 mark*

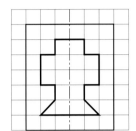

    (c)   See outer rectangle in diagram in (b)   *2 marks*

5. 48 ÷ 2 = 24, 60 − 48 = 12,
in 12 years' time, Graham will be 36 years old   *3 marks*

Tip: This problem needs to be broken down into stages. The three stages are shown above. Practice with similar problems will help the student to analyse what is required by the question.

6. (a)   40 = 25 + 15, B = 15   *2 marks*
    (b)   10 = 200 ÷ 20, T = 200   *2 marks*
    (c) $2(3 + 5)^2 = A$, 2 × 64 = 128, A = 128   *2 marks*

Tip: This question involves simple substitution into expressions. In (c) remember to square the contents of the bracket before multiplying by two.

7. (a)   6 × 9 × 3 = 54 × 3 = 162 cm³   *2 marks*
    (b)   (9 × 6) × 2 = 108 cm², (6 × 3) × 2 = 36 cm²,
          (9 × 3) × 2 = 54 cm², Total = 198 cm²   *2 marks*
    (c)   2 × 3 = 6 cubes could fit inside   *1 mark*

Tip: Students need to know how to calculate the volume of cubes, cuboids and some prisms. The unit of volume is a cubic measure such as cm³ or m³.

8. (a)   9; 36; 169   *3 marks*
    (b)   7; 8; 15   *3 marks*

9. (a)   *2 marks*

    (b)   Angles given in diagram in (a)   *3 marks*

Tip: Allow correct answers to 1° margin less than or greater than the ones given above.

10. (a)   5p, 2p, 1p   *2 marks*
    (b)   4 coins – 20p, 20p, 5p, 1p   *2 marks*

11. (a) Order of rotation is 1   *1 mark*
    (b)   *2 marks*

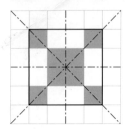

       see lines of symmetry on diagram;   *2 marks*
       order of rotation is 4   *1 mark*

12. (a) $7p + r$ *2 marks*
    (b) $m^2 + n^2$ *2 marks*
    (c) $t + a + y$ *2 marks*

     Tip: Simplifying expressions usually involves collecting like terms and removing brackets as well as raising powers.

13. (a) 20%   *1 mark*
    (b) 6   *1 mark*
    (c) 75%   *1 mark*
    (d) 3   *1 mark*

     Tip: The student needs to know how to convert from common to decimal to percentage fractions. A knowledge of the most common conversions is useful for quick recall.

14. (a) (−3, 5)   *2 marks*
    (b)   *2 marks*

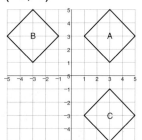

    (c) (3, −5)   *2 marks*

     Tip: This question involves coordinates in all four quadrants (which include negative values) and a reflection. A reflection is one form of transformation. The other three are translation (slide), enlargement (making bigger or smaller) and rotation (turn).

15. (a) £360;   *2 marks*
         £90   *2 marks*
    (b) £380;   *1 mark*
         £100   *2 marks*

     Tip: In order to find the amount spent in Week 3, in (b), it is necessary to work backwards by multiplying £95 by 4 to find the total spent for the month.

16. (a) Music   *2 marks*
    (b) English   *2 marks*
    (c) Music, $2 + 4 = 6$, $\frac{6}{30} = \frac{1}{5} = 20\%$ *2 marks*

17. (a) £60 – £45 = £15   *2 marks*
(b) $\frac{15}{60} = \frac{1}{4} = 25\%$ *2 marks*

18. (a) $3m = 15$ so $m = 5$ *1 mark*
(b) $2a = 8$ so $a = 4$ *2 marks*
(c) $10s - 15 = 25$, $10s = 40$ so $s = 4$ *2 marks*

Tip: These simple equations require a collection of like terms on one side and balancing (addition or subtraction of the same amount to both sides in order to simplify).

Total 90 Marks

Tier 4–6

Paper 2

1. (a)   *1 mark*

(b) $40\% = \frac{2}{5}$ *1 mark*
(c) $30\% = \frac{1}{5} + \frac{1}{10}$ *2 marks*

Tip: A knowledge of common fractions and percentage equivalence is required here. The student is helped by means of the shapes which are split into squares. The answer to (b) can be deduced from the shape in (a). Each square represents 20% or $\frac{1}{5}$.

2. (a) $n = 25$ *1 mark*
(b) $x + 15 = 20$ *1 mark*
(c) The equation is true because $n = 25$ and $x = 5$ from parts (a) and (b). Therefore $5 \times 5 = 25$.   *2 marks*

Tip: Here, the student is required to construct simple equations from the worded problem. In (c), the answers to the other parts are required in order to obtain the correct solution.

3. (a) ACD   *1 mark*
(b) Isosceles   *1 mark*
(c) $180° - (75° + 75°) = 30°$ *2 marks*
(d) $180° - (80° + 45°) = 55°$ *2 marks*
(e) The sum of the angles in a quadrilateral is 360°   *1 mark*

Tip: This question requires a knowledge of internal angles within triangles and quadrilaterals and in particular, the fact that the sum of the interior angles of a triangle is 180° and that of a quadrilateral is 360°.

4. (a) Area of rectangle is $5 \times 4 = 20$ cm^2;   *1 mark*
Area of triangle is $(4 \times 5) \div 2 = 10$ cm^2 *1 mark*
(b) Area of rectangle $= x \times y$ or xy cm^2 *1 mark*

Area of triangle = $\frac{1}{2}$ *xy* cm²   1 mark
Perimeter of rectangle = 2*x* + 2*y*   2 marks

Tip: Here students need to deduce formulae for the areas of rectangles and triangles and express them using the terms of algebra.

5. (a)   Shape B is a reflection of Shape A   1 mark
Shape C is a rotation of Shape A   1 mark
   (b)   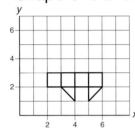   2 marks

Tip: A shape which has rotational symmetry can be turned about a point and will still look the same. Shape E has a rotational symmetry of the order 2 as it can be turned 180° about its centre and will still look the same.

6. (a)   0.5 + 0.8 = 1.3 or 0.8 + 0.5 = 1.3   2 marks
   (b)   0.5 x 0.8 = 0.4 or 0.8 x 0.5 = 0.4   2 marks
   (c)   0.5 x 0.1 x 1.0 = 0.05   3 marks

7. (a)   Spinner B;   1 mark
Probability = $\frac{1}{2}$ 1 mark
   (b)   40 times;   2 marks
There are not enough trials for either spinner in order for this conclusion to be made; also, Spinner A has been spun more times than B so the comparison would not be fair   2 marks

Tip: (a) is concerned with theoretical probability whereas (b) is experimental. The student needs to understand the concept of bias or unequal probabilities and also that, as the number of trials increases, the experimental will get closer to the theoretical.

8. (a)   5 x 5 = 25 cm²   1 mark
   (b)   Possible rectangles: 6 cm x 4 cm, 7 cm x 3 cm,
8 cm x 2 cm or 9 cm x 1 cm   2 marks
Possible areas: 24 cm², 21 cm², 16 cm² or 9 cm²   1 mark
   (c)   Answers will depend on the dimensions of the rectangle   3 marks

9. (a)   3*a* + 30;   1 mark
3*a* + 50 = 180, *a* = 50°   2 marks
   (b)   4*x* + 4;   2 marks
28 cm   2 marks

Tip: This is a good way of introducing students to algebraic expressions and finding their values using substitution. The problem is visual and therefore can be understood more easily.

10. (a)   96 pupils visit the factory;   2 marks
$\frac{1}{8}$ of 96 = 12, 12 pupils would like to work at the factory   2 marks
   (b) $\frac{1}{3}$ of 24 = 8, 24 − 8 = 16 pupils do not travel by bus   2 marks

11. (a) 30 pupils   *1 mark*

  (b) Probability green eyes = $\frac{5}{30}$ = $\frac{1}{6}$;   *1 mark*

    Probability brown hair = $\frac{20}{30}$ = $\frac{2}{3}$ *1 mark*

  (b) One reason to disagree is that twice as many of the pupils in 9J are girls, so it is likely that most brown haired pupils are girls;   *1 mark*

    $\frac{1}{3}$ of 20 = $6\frac{2}{3}$ so the answer 6 or 7 boys is acceptable   *2 marks*

12. (a) Brand A is the cheapest per litre   *1 mark*

  (b) A is now 27.5p per litre, B is now 28p per litre, C is $\frac{30}{750}$ x 1000 = 40p per litre, so Brand A is still the cheapest per litre   *2 marks*

  (b) Brand C is the most expensive per litre   *2 marks*

    Reasons may include: special flavours, loyalty to the company, preferred taste, not wanting to carry heavier bottle   *2 marks*

13. (a) 3(12 x 30) + 2(12 x 12) = 1080 + 288 = 1368 cm²;   *2 marks*

    1368 x 0.2 x 100 = 27360p = £273.60   *2 marks*

  (b) Volume of Box A = 12 x 30 x 12 = 4320 cm³

    Volume of Box B = 18 x 18 x 18 = 5832 cm³

    so Box B has the bigger volume   *3 marks*

14. (a) Sam will draw 4 more triangles   *1 mark*

  (b) Hexagon   *1 mark*

  (c) Base angles = (180° − 60°) ÷ 2 = 60°, so all angles are 60° making triangle equilateral   *2 marks*

  (d) Perimeter = 5 cm x 6 = 30 cm   *2 marks*

15. (a) Shape A is a scalene triangle with two acute angles and one obtuse angle   *3 marks*

  (b) Shape B is a pentagon with three right angles, two obtuse angles, straight sides and one pair of equal parallel sides   *3 marks*

Total 90 Marks

Tier 5–7

Paper 1

1. (a) 5p, 2p, 1p — *2 marks*
   (b) 4 coins – 20p, 20p, 5p, 1p — *2 marks*

2. (a) Order of rotation is 1 — *1 mark*
   (b) — *2 marks*

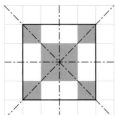

   see lines of symmetry on diagram; — *2 marks*
   order of rotation is 4 — *1 mark*

3. (a) $7p + r$ — *1 mark*
   (b) $m^2 + n^2$ — *2 marks*
   (c) $t + a + y$ — *2 marks*

   Tip: Simplifying expressions usually involves collecting like terms and removing brackets as well as raising powers.

4. (a) 20% — *1 mark*
   (b) 6 — *1 mark*
   (c) 75% — *1 mark*
   (d) 3 — *1 mark*

   Tip: The student needs to know how to convert from common to decimal to percentage fractions. A knowledge of the most common conversions is useful for quick recall.

5. (a) (–3, 5) — *2 marks*
   (b) — *2 marks*

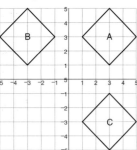

   (c) (3, –5) — *2 marks*

   Tip: This question involves coordinates in all four quadrants (which include negative values) and a reflection. A reflection is one form of transformation. The other three are translation (slide), enlargement (making bigger or smaller) and rotation (turn).

6. (a) £360; — *2 marks*
   £90 — *2 marks*
   (b) £380; — *1 mark*
   £100 — *2 marks*

Tip: In order to find the amount spent in Week 3, in (b), it is necessary to work backwards by multiplying £95 by 4 to find the total spent for the month.

7. (a) Music   *2 marks*
   (b) English   *2 marks*
   (c) Music, $2 + 4 = 6$, $\frac{6}{30} = \frac{1}{5} = 20\%$ *2 marks*

Tip: Each boy is worth 10% of the boys' total. Each girl is worth 5% of the girls' total.

8. (a) £60 – £45 = £15   *2 marks*
   (b) $\frac{15}{60} = \frac{1}{4} = 25\%$ *2 marks*

9. (a) $3m = 15$ so $m = 5$ *1 mark*
   (b) $2a = 8$ so $a = 4$ *1 mark*
   (c) $10s - 15 = 25$, $10s = 40$ so $s = 4$ *2 marks*

Tip: These simple equations require a collection of like terms on one side and balancing (addition or subtraction of the same amount to both sides in order to simplify).

10. (a) Perimeter of *T*: $4b + 6a$ *1 mark*
         Perimeter of *V*: $4b + 4a + 2c$ *1 mark*
   (b) Area of T: $3a \times 2b = 6ab$ *2 marks*

11. (a)   *1 mark*

```
0          1/2          1
|-+-+-+-+-+-+-+-+-+-+-|
              ↑
             3/5
```

   (b) $\frac{3}{5} - \frac{3}{10} = \frac{6}{10} - \frac{3}{10} = \frac{3}{10}$ *1 mark*
   (c) $1\frac{3}{4} + \frac{5}{8} = 1\frac{6}{8} + \frac{5}{8} = 1\frac{11}{8} = 2\frac{3}{8}$ *2 marks*

Tip: In (c) it is necessary to first find a common denominator (eighths) and then convert the improper or top heavy fraction into a mixed number.

12. (a) $0.2 + 0.5 = 0.7$ *1 mark*
   (b) $0.2 \times 100 = 20$ *1 mark*
   (c) $\frac{1}{4} + 0.5 = \frac{3}{4}$ *1 mark*
   (d) $2 - 1\frac{4}{5} = \frac{1}{5}$ *1 mark*

13. (a)   *1 mark*

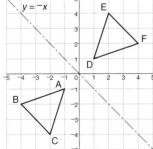

   (b) A = (–1, –1)   B = (–4, –2)   C = (–2, –4)   *3 marks*
   (c) See reflection in (a)   *2 marks*
         D = (1, 1)   E = (2, 4)   F = (4, 2)   *3 marks*

Tip: The line $y = -x$ is a straight line which cuts the origin at 45°. The line $y = x$ also cuts the origin at 45° but slopes the other way (forwards).

14. (a) $\frac{1}{7}$; *1 mark*

$\frac{3}{7}$; *1 mark*

0 *1 mark*

(b) $\frac{6}{12} = \frac{1}{2}$ *2 marks*

Tip: In (a) the value of the coins does not affect the chances. In (b), the student needs to work out all of the possible combinations before arriving at the answer.

15. (a) *3 marks*

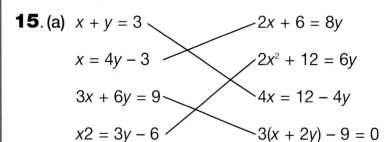

$x + y = 3$ — $4x = 12 - 4y$

$x = 4y - 3$ — $2x^2 + 12 = 6y$

$3x + 6y = 9$ — $3(x + 2y) - 9 = 0$

$x2 = 3y - 6$ — $2x + 6 = 8y$

(b) $5t + 10 \le 15$, $5t \le 5$ so $t \le 1$; *2 marks*

$\frac{a}{5} - 1 > 6$, $\frac{a}{5} > 7$ so $a > 35$ *2 marks*

Tip: One of each pair of equivalent equations is a simplified version of the other. The inequalities are solved in the same way as equations (i.e. by balancing both sides in order to obtain the unknown term in a simplified state).

16. (a) Area of zone $R = a \times b = ab$ *1 mark*

Area of zone $T = \frac{a}{2}(b + 5)$ *2 marks*

(b) Area of zone $T = \frac{20}{2}(b + 5)$

$10b + 50 = 140$, $10b = 90$, $b = 9$ m; *2 marks*

Area of playground $= \underline{a} \times (\underline{b} + \underline{b} + 5) = 20(9 + 9 + 5) = 460 \ m^2$ *2 marks*

17. (a) *2 marks*

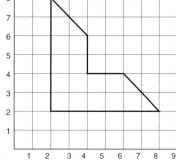

(b) *2 marks*

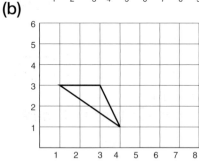

Tip: In (b) the shape will be made smaller as the scale factor is fractional.

Total 90 Marks

Tier 5–7

Paper 2

1. (a) $5 \times 5 = 25 \text{ cm}^2$ *1 mark*
   (b) Possible rectangles: 6 cm x 4 cm, 7 cm x 3 cm,
       8 cm x 2 cm or 9 cm x 1 cm   *1 mark*
       Possible areas: 24 cm², 21 cm², 16 cm² or 9 cm²   *1 mark*
   (c) Answers will depend on the dimensions of the rectangle .   *3 marks*

2. (a) $3a + 30$;   *1 mark*
       $3a + 50 = 180$, $a = 50°$ *2 marks*
   (b) $4x + 4$;   *2 marks*
       28 cm   *1 mark*

> *Tip: This is a good way of introducing students to algebraic expressions and finding their values using substitution. The problem is visual and therefore can be understood more easily.*

3. (a) 96 pupils visit the factory;   *2 marks*
       $\frac{1}{8}$ of 96 = 12, 12 pupils would like to work at the factory   *1 mark*
   (b) $\frac{1}{3}$ of 24 = 8, 24 − 8 = 16 pupils do not travel by bus   *2 marks*

> *Tip: This problem needs to be read carefully more than once. In order to answer (a) students need to appreciate that $\frac{1}{4}$ of the pupils prefer the office and therefore multiply 24 by 4 to get 96 pupils in all. Also, it is useful to know that $12\frac{1}{2}\%$ is equivalent to $\frac{1}{8}$.*

4. (a) 30 pupils   *1 mark*
   (b) Probability green eyes = $\frac{5}{30} = \frac{1}{6}$;   *1 mark*
       Probability brown hair = $\frac{20}{30} = \frac{2}{3}$ *1 mark*
   (c) One reason to disagree is that twice as many of the pupils in 9J are girls, so it is likely that most brown haired pupils are girls;   *1 mark*
       $\frac{1}{3}$ of 20 = $6\frac{2}{3}$ so the answer 6 or 7 boys is acceptable   *2 marks*

> *Tip: In (a) an easy mistake here is to add the numbers in both tables, giving 60 pupils instead of the correct 30. This problem is about experimental or estimated probability where the probability fraction is produced from actual results.*

5. (a) Brand A is the cheapest per litre   *1 mark*
   (b) A is now 27.5p per litre, B is now 28p per litre,
       C is $\frac{30}{750}$ x 1000 = 40p per litre, so Brand A is still the cheapest per litre   *2 marks*
   (c) Brand C is the most expensive per litre   *2 marks*
       Reasons may include: special flavours, loyalty to the company, preferred taste, not wanting to carry heavier bottle   *1 mark*

> *Tip: This problem relates to the unit costs of branded goods where the size of the product often masks the real cost.*

6. (a) $3(12 \times 30) + 2(12 \times 12) = 1080 + 288 = 1368 \text{ cm}^2$;   *2 marks*
       1368 x 0.2 x 100 = 27360p = £273.60   *2 marks*
   (b) Volume of Box A = 12 x 30 x 12 = 4320 cm³

Volume of Box B = 18 x 18 x 18 = 5832 cm³
so Box B has the bigger volume   *2 marks*

Tip: In (a) it is easiest to find the surface area of one rectangle (not the ends) and then multiply by three.

7. (a) Sam will draw 4 more triangles   *1 mark*
   (b) Hexagon   *1 mark*
   (c) Base angles = (180° − 60°) ÷ 2 = 60°, so all angles are 60°
        making triangle equilateral   *2 marks*
   (d) Perimeter = 5 cm x 6 = 30 cm   *1 mark*

Tip: For (a) the student needs to know that the angle at the centre of the circle is 360°.

8. (a) Shape A is a scalene triangle with two acute angles and one
        obtuse angle   *2 marks*
   (b) Shape B is a pentagon with three right angles, two obtuse
        angles, straight sides and one pair of equal parallel sides   *2 marks*

Tip: To gain full marks, at least four of the terms should be used in each part.

9. (a) B = $\frac{3}{8}$, C = $\frac{5}{32}$, D = $\frac{3}{32}$ *3 marks*
   (b) Piece B   *1 mark*
   (c) $\frac{3}{8} + \frac{1}{4} + \frac{3}{32} = \frac{12}{32} + \frac{8}{32} + \frac{3}{32} = \frac{23}{32}$ *2 marks*

Tip: (c) requires knowledge of common denominators for the addition of fractions.

10. (a) 6:5 = 18:15, 18 + 15 = 33 pupils   *2 marks*
    (b) 15:15 = 1:1   *2 marks*

Tip: In (a) the answer is arrived at by first multiplying 6 by 3 to give the number of girls. Multiplying 5 by 3 (the same amount) then gives the number of boys.

11. (a) $\frac{3}{4} = \frac{6}{x} = \frac{6}{8}$, so $x = 8$ *1 mark*
    (b) $\frac{3}{4} = \frac{x}{18} = \frac{13.5}{18}$, so $x = 13.5$ *1 mark*
    (c) $\frac{3.5}{4} = \frac{x}{10} = \frac{8.75}{10}$, so $x = 8.75$ *1 mark*

Tip: This question is about equivalence and multiplying/dividing both numerator and denominator by the same amount in order to obtain the unknown x.

12. (a) Boys: mean = 205 ÷ 10 = 20.5, range = 30 − 12 = 18   *3 marks*
        Girls: mean = 164 ÷ 10 = 16.4, range = 24 − 6 = 18   *3 marks*
    (b) Possible answers: the sample is too small to draw this
         conclusion, the sample may not be random (e.g. boys and
         girls of different ages), the experiment may not have been
         conducted under the same conditions for both boys and girls   *1 mark*

Tip: This experiment is an easy one for the student to try for himself/herself and obtain data. The range and mean could then be compared with the results in the question.

13. (a) $4a$ *1 mark*
   (b) Area of the square = $4a \times 4a = 16a^2$
       Area of one CD = πa^2, so area of four CDs = $4\pi a^2$
       Therefore area of waste = $16a^2 - 4\pi a^2$ *2 marks*

14. (a)

Pairs	% of Boys	Number of Boys
1	20%	4
2	20%	4
3	10%	2
4	40%	8
5	10%	2
6	0%	0

5 marks

   (b) $(4 \times 1) + (4 \times 2) + (2 \times 3) + (8 \times 4) + (2 \times 5) + (0 \times 6) = 60$ pairs   *2 marks*
   (c) Mean number of pairs $60 \div 20 = 3$ pairs   *2 marks*

   Tip: In (c) the student is required to find the mean of a frequency
   distribution. This is calculated by multiplying the number of pairs of
   shoes by the number of boys as shown in (b) and then dividing by the
   number of boys.

15. (a)

B	1	5	9	13	17	21	$4n - 3$
C	1	4	9	16	25	36	n^2
D	0	7	26	63	124	215	$n^3 - 1$

3 marks

   (b)
   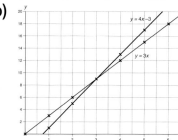

   $x = 3, y = 9$ *2 marks*

   Tip: Points for the straight line equations for (b) can be obtained from
   the table in (a): $3n$ and $4n - 3$.

16. (a) 6.4 cm and 4.8 cm   *2 marks*
   (b) $\frac{14}{8} = 1.75$, $6 \times 1.75 = 10.5$, so $x = 10.5$ cm   *2 marks*

17. (a) $3x < 6$, so $x < 2$ *2 marks*
   (b) $x = 5, y = 0$ *3 marks*

   Tip: For (b), in order to solve this simultaneous equation, it is
   necessary to make the coefficients of either x or y the same before
   subtracting one equation from the other.
       $2x - y = 10$ (1)
       $x + 3y = 5$ (2)
       multiply (2) by 2
       $2x + 6y = 10$ (3)
       subtract (3) from (1)
       $-7y = 0$
       $y = 0$
       substituting $y = 0$ into (1), $2x = 10$. Therefore $x = 5$.

Total 90 Marks

Mental Maths Test 1

1. 0.3	11. 11.7	21. $\frac{1}{16}$
2. 625	12. 3.5 cm	22. 161
3. 230 cm	13. 14 cm²	23. 20
4. 121	14. $x = -1$	24. 160 cm³
5. 1000403	15. $\frac{1}{2}$	25. £120
6. $3y - 10$	16. 5400	26. 6
7. East	17. $12x^2 + 6x$	27. 45 miles
8. 1 hr 12 min	18. 19	28. 21, 22, 23
9. £6.00	19. −90	29. 240
10. $\frac{1}{8}$	20. 512	30. 12, 13

1 mark each question

Total 30 Marks

Mental Maths Test 2

1. 125	11. 30	21. 12.25 pm
2. 9	12. 12	22. 37
3. 0.45	13. 18	23. 6.3 cm
4. 409	14. 8 or 28	24. 120°
5. $7y - w$	15. 50 cm³	25. $\frac{3}{50}$
6. −7	16. 35%	26. 52
7. 70	17. 4	27. 23
8. 10	18. 45°	28. 6.9
9. £64	19. 25%	29. 30 sec
10. 15	20. 120	30. Parallel

1 mark each question

Total 30 Marks

Mark scheme for KS3 Maths

How to calculate your level

To find out how well you have done in the practice papers:

- Add together your marks for Paper 1, Paper 2 and the Mental Maths test. (Possible Total = 210)
- Use the table below to find your level;
- Make sure you look at the right tier of papers.

Level	Tier 3–5 papers	Tier 4–6 papers	Tier 5–7 papers
N (means no level achieved)	0–25	0–35	0–45
2	26–34		
3	35–50	36–42	
4	51–140	43–60	46–50
5	141 or more	61–150	51–70
6		151 or more	71–160
7			161 or more